Knowledge Management in High Risk Industries

Philippe Fauquet-Alekhine

Knowledge Management in High Risk Industries

Coping with Skills Drain

palgrave
macmillan

Philippe Fauquet-Alekhine
INTRA Robotics
Avoine, France

ISBN 978-3-030-49212-0 ISBN 978-3-030-49213-7 (eBook)
https://doi.org/10.1007/978-3-030-49213-7

This Palgrave Macmillan imprint is published by the registered company Springer Nature Switzerland AG
The registered company address is: Gewerbestrasse 11, 6330 Cham, Switzerland

Foreword

This book presents a new method to train personnel in high-tech, high-risk industries. The method has proven its efficiency, with measurable results, and is explained here in sufficient pedagogic detail to be applied in various situations.

The method is fit, more efficient and realistic. It is well-fit to each specific case because it feeds on detailed empirical evidence from the very contexts where it will be applied. It is efficient than current methods because it gathers the expert knowledge and know-how with a new, more faithful and more detailed technique, using first-person video capture and analysis (Subjective Evidence-Based Ethnography). Finally, it is realistic because it takes into account the actual constraints of training in high-risk industries, including informal know-how, rare events, teamwork, shifts, simulator planning, etc. Indeed, the author is not only a brilliant scholar (with two PhDs) but also a seasoned practitioner who has been in charge of designing, running and evaluating training systems (including full-scale simulators) in the nuclear industry for many years. This is a rare and powerful combination, and the author, in sympathy with users, made the book short and clear.

The models used combine the best theories of four different traditions: French ergonomics, Russian activity theory, Californian distributed cognition and Japanese knowledge management (of which the author also provides a digest for those unfamiliar). The method is illustrated with actual applications. Well-designed tables and graphs provide powerful aids to the reader.

In short, a book that will be very useful for practitioners, experts and academics.

Professor S. Lahlou
Director at the Institute for Advanced Study
Paris, France

Chair of Psychology, Department
of Psychological & Behavioural Science
London School of Economics
London, UK

Acknowledgements The author thanks Electricité de France for financial support. The author thanks, for fruitful exchanges, the members of the Institute of Social Psychology, of the Department of Psychological & Behavioural Science and of the SEBE-Lab (London School of Economics & Political Science), especially Professor S. Lahlou and Professor M. Bauer. The author also thanks Professor Yuri I. Aleksandrov (Higher School of Economics, Faculty of Social Sciences, School of Psychology, Moscow, Russia) and Professor Granry (Hospital University of Angers, France) for collaboration and relevant advice.

About This Book

Dealing with the social phenomenon of the "skills drain", retired workers leaving companies *en masse* sometimes even before the recruitment of newcomers and consequently impeding classic training through mentoring, managers are seeking innovative solutions to train new employees and ensure a satisfactory level of competencies, especially in high-risk industries. This led to questions to which the present book aims at offering solutions: What should be transferred from experienced workers to novices through training in the current social context of deteriorated mentoring within complex socio-technical systems? How to select what should be transferred? How to access experienced workers' competencies?

Based on a solid literature review and experiments, two innovative validated models are presented:

- the Knowledge–Know-How–Skills model (KKHS model) which helps to clarify how competencies are elaborated and what can be transferred,
- the Square of PErceived ACtion model (SPEAC model) describing how to put successfully competencies in action.

Within the Cognitive Task Analysis paradigm, a protocol is then presented in the line of Subjective Evidence-Based Ethnography (SEBE) methods. It combines first-person recordings of the workers' activity by subcams (miniaturized cameras mounted on spectacles) and interviews.

The theoretical aspects underpinning the protocol are explained for a better use of the protocol and its implementation is fully described.

Examples of applications are given for the nuclear industry and in medicine, demonstrating the efficiency of the protocol to access what makes competencies of experienced workers and how this data can be used to improve performance through training. An example of its application in schools is also presented, showing that it is not restricted to the occupational area.

How models and protocol integrate the Knowledge Management paradigm is also exposed.

We suggest that companies could benefit from the protocol presented in this book to improve their professional training. Four key points make the protocol of interest: its efficiency at detecting knowledge and know-how necessary to perform an activity, its low cost, the good workers' acceptance and the performance improvement it provides.

Contents

About the Author

Philippe Fauquet-Alekhine is Scientific Director at INTRA Robotics, in charge of international scientific projects and of the training programme. Beforehand, he was Human Factors Consultant & Researcher at Chinon Nuclear Power Plant (Electricité de France), expert in Innovative Development for Operational Professionalization, member of the Laboratory for Research in Science of Energy (France, Web Site: www.hayka-kultura.org), member of the SEBE-Lab at the LSE (UK, Web Site: www.SEBE-Lab.net).

Doctor in Physics Science (University Pierre & Marie Curie, Paris, France), Work Psychologist (M.Sc. from the Conservatoire des Arts & Métiers, Paris, France), doctor in Behavioural Psychology (London School of Economics & Political Science, UK), Philippe Fauquet-Alekhine is author of several scientific articles and books. He has more than 20-year experience in work activity analysis and research applied to human performance within high-risk industries. He contributes to researches and interventions in firms regarding the study of human in work situation, work organization, management; he collaborated to research in psycho-sociology at the Institute of Social Psychology and in the Department of Psychological & Behavioural Science (LSE, London, UK), and also at the Hospital of Paris, Angers and Toulouse (France). His scientific productions especially address the analysis of work activity, its modalities and contributions and its application in the industrial environment. They also concern sides that are more specific as the psycho-linguistic approach for the analysis of operational communication, or cognitive aspects of non-simulated work activities or of learning and training on simulator. For the industrial field, he investigates aerospace, aeronautics (civil and military), navy, nuclear industry and medicine.

Involved in the pedagogical conception of experimental training on simulator, he co-elaborates new scenarios based on shared experimental observations or by taking advantage of his 4 years of experience as a nuclear power plant safety expert, trained as reactor pilot in accidental situations and involved in exercises of crisis management.

Philippe Fauquet-Alekhine edited:

- *Améliorer la pratique professionnelle par la simulation*, Fauquet-Alekhine, Ph., & Pehuet, N. (2011) Editions Octares, Toulouse, France.
- *Simulation Training: Fundamentals and Applications*, Fauquet-Alekhine, Ph., & Pehuet, N. (2015) Springer Verlag, Berlin, Germany.

Abbreviations

AT	Activity Theory
DCog	Distributed Cognition
EDF	Electricité de France
EDF SA	French EDF company
K&KH	Knowledge & Know-How (model)
KKHS	Knowledge, Know-How & Skills
KM	Knowledge Management
KMC	Knowledge Management Cycle
MO	Modus Operandi, procedure
NPP	Nuclear Power Plant
PjB	Pre Job Briefing
RIW	Replay Interview
ROS	Real Operating Situation
SAT	Systematic Approach Training
SEBE	Subjective Evidence-Based Ethnography
SECI	Socialization–Externalization–Combination–Internalization (model)
SimS	Simulated Situation
SPEAC	Square of PErceived ACtion
TOTE	Test–Operate–Test–Exit (model)
WANO	World Association of Nuclear Operators

Symbols and Units

Symbol	Quantity	Units
df	degree of freedom	None
M	mean value	Depending on the measured quantity
N	number of a sample	None
r	correlation coefficient	None
R	determination coefficient	None
SD	standard deviation	Depending on the measured quantity
p	significance	None
t	t de Student	None
α	Cronbach's alpha	None
χ^2	KHI-square coefficient	None

List of Figures

List of Tables

CHAPTER 1

Introduction: Competencies Transference and Skills Drain

Abstract This chapter describes the rationale of the book from the industrial standpoint: it describes the current occupational need in complex socio-technical systems. The occupational context, the training context and the social context are briefly described and the major weaknesses are highlighted leading to the concept of "skills drain"; the related difficulties regarding occupational training are described. It shows that the issue is thus to know: What should be transferred from experienced workers to novices through training in the current social context of deteriorated mentoring within complex socio-technical systems? This relates to correlate questions: How to select what should be transferred? How to access experienced workers' competencies?

Keywords Skills drain · Competencies · Training · Occupational

High-risk technical industries are usually elaborated from a simple technical idea for basic needs. For example, nuclear production consists in producing electric energy from nuclear energy. That is to say taking the simple concept of the fission of atoms, obtain heat, then use it to transform liquid (usually water) into pressurized gas and use the energy to power a turbine. This turbine is coupled to an alternator which produces electricity. Unfortunately, the technical accomplishment of an apparently simple idea remains complex and leads to the elaboration of a complex

P. Fauquet-Alekhine, *Knowledge Management in High Risk Industries*, https://doi.org/10.1007/978-3-030-49213-7_1

technical system that may give rise to safety problems (Amalberti, 1996, 2001; Reason, 1990, 2008, 2016).

Men and women are required to help this complex technical system operate, within an organization which in itself is complex. The complex technical system therefore becomes a complex socio-technical system. The issues of safety and reliability thus remain crucial from a technical standpoint but also from organizational and human standpoints. Amalberti (1996) speaks of resident pathogenic agents within the socio-technical system "like a virus that would become active during any favorable context". De la Garza and Fadier (2007) warn us about socio-technical systems that weaken over time (see also Heimann, 2005). This may be induced, among other factors, by the ignorance of certain risks, operation and production constraints and a tolerance within the organization that accepts that certain limits are exceeded (this is the normalization of deviation suggested by Vaughan, 1996, 2005).

The efficiency and the improvement of safety and reliability of such complex socio-technical systems are based in part on the professionalism of the workers. This is elaborated through professional training within a professionalization strategy. "Efficiency is gained by reducing the time it takes to reach a specified level of learning, and effectiveness is gained by achieving better results in performing the tasks learned" (Parush et al., 2002: 320).

They may be insidious such as those induced by the high level of requirements these sorts of industries demand thus leading to difficulties in applying overly complex procedures when compared to the basic information needed to perform the task: five lines to explain the core of the task and how to perform it, two pages to warn the operator about potential problems, two more pages listing what is forbidden, then four and a half pages describing the steps to be taken—all this rather than half a page of basic information regarding the action (see, for example, Fauquet-Alekhine, 2015: 5). This is the result of requirements and explicit or implicit regulations that constrain actions and interactions within the socio-technical system (Béguin & Clot, 2004; Bruno & Munoz, 2010; Hasu & Engestrom, 2000), combined with additional information resulting from feedback of the safety event analysis and pollution by operating details due to the belief that know-how and skills can be put on paper. The resulting procedure may be four times more pages than what is strictly necessary to understand how to carry out the task. This leads workers to blindly apply the procedure rather than trying to understand the application of the procedures or making intelligent use of the tools that are at their disposition (Butterworth, 2010). Dubar and Mercier (2002: 182), when presenting an analysis of experienced workers' competencies at the French nuclear operator EDF, complained: "we write everything, we have to write everything and of course we must write competencies". A more recent analysis carried out at a French nuclear power plant (Fauquet-Alekhine & Boucherand, 2011: 36) aiming at identifying organizational resource and difficulties suggested that professional training had to be restructured: "rethinking the integration of know-how in professional training is necessary, and prior rethinking of access to this know-how is necessary: the 'all-in-procedure' is not a solution".

If workers are not educated to deal with such difficulties during the training period, then the associated know-how can be developed through mentoring,[1] a period during which knowledge, know-how and operating skills are expected to improve or at least develop. But is it possible? Does it happen? The answer must be discussed by taking an emerging social factor of the past decade into account: the skills drain.

Western European industries, which include technological high-risk industries, must now come to terms with the problem of the skills drain (Fauquet-Alekhine, 2016; Fitzpatrick, 2011; Le Bellu, 2016; Manner, 2012; Newcombe, 2013; Richardson, 2012) due to retirement. This reduces the contribution of experienced workers for tutorial and periods of mentoring. This social phenomenon is combined with an established depletion of professionalization in a work context with drastic requirements that make the tools shaped and sized by operational and safety standards (Béguin & Clot, 2004; Bruno & Munoz, 2010; Hasu & Engestrom, 2000). The combination results in increasing difficulties for workers to fully apply procedures or use tools efficiently. The skills drain, not to be confused with "brain drain", may have a consequence on industrial safety (Murphy, Bennett, Hoile, Borte, & Smith, 2010; Turner, 2013).

These findings point out the principal difficulties encountered by high-risk industries (skills drain, reduced contribution of experienced workers as a tutor and for mentoring, depletion of professionalization, tools shaped and sized by operational and safety standards and

[1] "mentoring" is the English translation for "compagnonnage" in French.

regulations, difficulties for workers to perform a comprehensive application of the procedures or a clever use of tools), both in the field of operating and in the field of training. Coping with these difficulties, or at least adapting them, could bring great benefits for the companies in terms of performance and for the employees' well-being and health at work (e.g. see Clot, 2008).

However, this is not so easy. The overall problem comes from opposite considerations: the contribution of experienced workers is fundamental to the newcomers' mentoring periods but most of the experienced workers have retired or are about to be retired. If this is not the case, their involvement in high-stakes work activities and on-call activities makes them unavailable for the training of newcomers.

The present book aims at providing an efficient solution to this issue by tackling the following question:

What should be transferred from experienced workers to novices through training in the current social context of deteriorated mentoring within complex socio-technical systems? This relates to correlate questions: How to select what should be transferred? How to access experienced workers' competencies?

Firstly, these questions imply defining what we are referring to when we use "competent", "competencies" and what their links with knowledge, know-how and skills are. This is analysed through a literature review presented in Chapter 2 "What Do We Transfer?".

Secondly, these questions entail the need to better understand the way in which competencies may successfully be summoned and used to achieve an individual or collective activity in operating situations at work and how, when summoned in situation, they may be characterized for further training purposes. This is analysed through a literature review presented in Chapter 3 "Competencies Need Action".

Thirdly, when defined and characterized, the concern is then to apply the resulting material and conclusions efficiently in the framework of a professionalization process within complex socio-technical systems. This is elaborated and described in Chapter 4 "Refining Competencies Identification Through Digital Ethnography" under the name "SEBE/SPEAC protocol". The SEBE/SPEAC protocol thus aims at identifying relevant knowledge and know-how that are necessary for performing a work activity with success and at providing exhaustive input data for the related occupational training.

Chapter 5 gives examples of application and discusses the acceptance of the protocol by workers. It also provides pieces of advice about the implementation of the solutions and about practitioners' training in order to apply the solutions.

References

Amalberti, R. (1996). *La conduite des systèmes à risques*. Paris: PUF.

Amalberti, R. (2001). The paradoxes of almost totally safe transportation systems. *Safety Science, 37*(2–3), 109–126.

Béguin, P., & Clot, Y. (2004). Situated action in the development of activity. *Electronic review @ctivités, 1*(2), 50–63. www.activites.org.

Bruno, S., & Munoz, G. (2010). Education and interactivism: Levels of interaction influencing learning processes. *New Ideas in Psychology, 28*(3), 365–379.

Butterworth, H. H. (2010). *Human performance tools*. Xcel Energy report, ref: FP-PA-HU-02. http://pbadupws.nrc.gov/docs/ML1021/ML102120052.pdf.

Clot, Y. (2008). Occupational health: Models, measures and actions. *Revue européenne de psychologie appliqué, 58*, 297–299.

De la Garza, C., & Fadier, E. (2007). Le retour d'expérience en tant que cadre théorique pour l'analyse de l'activité et de la conception sûre. *@ctivités, 4*(1), 188–197.

Dubar, C., & Mercier, D. (2002). Entretien biographique comme outil d'analyse des compétences: l'exemple des agents EDF-GDF en fin de carrière. In H. Y. Meynaud & X. Marc (Eds.), *Entreprise et société: dialogues de chercheur(e)s à EDF* (pp. 161–200). Paris: L'Harmattan.

Fauquet-Alekhine, Ph. (2015). *Evaluation des RPS- AEE-ANA-RE* [Assessment of psycho-social risks, Dept. AEE, Team ANA, profession Team Manager]. Internal Report EDF ref.: D.5170/DIR/NED.15.002 ind 00.

Fauquet-Alekhine, Ph. (2016). Subjective ethnographic protocol for work activity analysis and occupational training improvement. *British Journal of Applied Science & Technology, 12*(5), 1–16, Article no.BJAST.21632.

Fauquet-Alekhine, Ph., & Boucherand, A. (2011). *Analyse Socio-Organisationnelle & Humaine: étude des causes profondes – Chinon 2010–2011*. EDF Internal report ref: D.5170/DIR/NED/11.005.

Fitzpatrick, T. (2011). Northern Ireland to address jobs and skills drain. *Construction News*. http://www.cnplus.co.uk/news/northern-ireland-to-address-jobs-and-skills-drain/8618647.article.

Hasu, M., & Engestrom, Y. (2000). Measurement in action: An activity-theoretical perspective on producer/user interaction. *International Journal of Human-Computer Studies, 53*, 61–89.

Heimann, L. (2005). Repeated failures in the management of high risk technologies. *European Management Journal, 3*(1), 105–117.

Le Bellu, S. (2016). Learning the secrets of the craft through the real-time experience of experts: Capturing and transferring experts' tacit knowledge to novices. *PISTES*, 18–1. http://pistes.revues.org/4685.

Manner, D. (2012). UK industry suffering skills shortage. *ElectronicsWeekly.com*. http://www.electronicsweekly.com/Articles/12/11/2012/54981/uk-industry-suffering-skills-shortage-says-eef.htm.

Murphy, B., Bennett, S., Hoile, S., Borte, U., & Smith, C. (2010). Next generation, skills for new build nuclear. *Renaissance Nuclear skills series, 2*. http://www.cogent-ssc.com/research/Publications/Renaissance2.pdf.

Newcombe, T. (2013). UK skills shortage threatens food and drink manufacturing competitiveness, reveals report. *HRmagazine.co.uk*. http://www.hrmagazine.co.uk/hro/news/1075796/uk-skills-shortage-threatens-food-drink-manufacturing-competitiveness-reveals-report.

Parush, A., Hamm, H., & Shtub, A. (2002). Learning histories in simulation-based teaching: The effects on self-learning and transfer. *Computers & Education, 39*, 319–332.

Reason, J. (1990). *Human error*. New York: Cambridge university press.

Reason, J. (2008). *The human contribution: Unsafe acts, Accidents and Heroic Recoveries*. Farnham, UK: Ashgate.

Reason, J. (2016). *Managing the risks of organizational accidents*. London: Routledge.

Richardson, H. (2012). *Warning over shortage of engineering graduates*. BBC Education & Family. http://www.bbc.co.uk/news/education-19760351.

Turner, P. (2013). Solve the skills shortage and protect asset safety. *EngineerLive.com*. http://www.engineerlive.com/Process-Engineer/Automation_Control/Solve_the_skills_shortage_and_protect_asset_safety/23423/.

Vaughan, D. (1996). *The Challenger launch decision, risky technology, culture And deviance at NASA*. Chicago: The Chicago University Press.

Vaughan, D. (2005). System effects: On slippery slopes, repeating negative pattern, and learning from mistake? In H. W. Starbuck & M. Farjoun, *Organizations at the limit: Lessons from the Columbia disaster* (pp. 41–59). Malden: Blackwell.

CHAPTER 2

What Do We Transfer?

Abstract This chapter examines through a review how the literature makes the link between knowledge, know-how, skills and competencies. It suggests that competencies must be mobilized in order to perform an activity and that this mobilization is multi-factorial and occurs when in action. It suggests a way to synthetize the conclusions of the review through the Knowledge–Know-How–Skills model (KKHS model) depicting the interrelationship between the three notions, demonstrates the robustness of the model and exposes how it integrates the Knowledge Management paradigm.

Keywords Knowledge · Know-how · Skills · Competencies · Knowledge Management · Knowledge–Know-How–Skills model

2.1 Defining Competencies: The KKHS Model

Here the question of defining knowledge, know-how, skills and competencies is addressed. It is common to hear trainers or trainees, workers or managers use these words indifferently. It is also difficult to form a clear idea about these concepts when reading the scientific literature as shown hereinafter.

A team at the European Centre for the Development of Vocational Training (Luxembourg), Winterton and co-workers (2006), published a report giving a detailed description of what—according to their

P. Fauquet-Alekhine, *Knowledge Management in High Risk Industries*, https://doi.org/10.1007/978-3-030-49213-7_2

analysis—knowledge, skill and competence are, although their bibliographic review has put the contribution of ex-Soviet researchers to one side in favour of West European and Anglo-Saxon researchers. The same shortfall arises in the review of Boucher, Bonjour, and Grabot (2007). These reviews suggest that the literature distinguishes two kinds of learning processes: (i) single-loop learning related to knowledge based on existing premises so as to solve specific problems (Dodgson, 1993) and (ii) double-loop learning which aims to establish new premises such as mental models and perspectives (Argyris & Schön, 1974, 1978; Bateson, 1973). Knowledge development is part of a learning process (Nonaka & Takeuchi, 1995) which may concern a cognitive dimension (understanding and the use of new concepts) and/or a behavioural dimension (the physical ability to act) (Garvin, 1993), the interaction of which within a social system leads to organizational learning (Senge, 1990). Knowledge includes both declarative knowledge (explicit, factual knowledge), including theory and concepts, and tacit knowledge resulting mainly from experience (Eraut, 2000; Polanyi, 1958, 1967; Polanyi & Sen, 2009; Wagner & Sternberg, 1986), which is sometimes difficult to put into words, such as using a ruler to measure the axis of a pump. Furthermore, the work of Wenger (1998) showed that information at work is context-sensitive and only makes sense if it is maintained by a community of practice, a group of people involved in a common concern giving rise to shared actions on a regular basis. According to Wenger, communities of practice are a necessary condition for the sustainability of tacit knowledge.

Regarding skills, Winterton and co-workers quote Proctor and Dutta (1995). According to Winterton et al., "the most authoritative text on skill acquisition and performance", who define skill as "goal-directed, well-organised behaviour that is acquired through practice and performed with economy of effort", distinguishing perceptual skills, response selection skills, motor skills and problem-solving skills. Before them, Rasmussen (1983) suggested skill-based behaviour as "highly integrated patterns of behaviour", related to "sensory-motor performance during acts" following intention and happening without conscious control.

Defining "competence", however, is less easy. According to Winterton and co-workers, "there is such confusion and debate about the concept of competence that it is impossible to identify or impute a coherent theory or to arrive at a definition capable of accommodating and reconciling all the different ways the term is used". Moreover, some authors use "competency" instead of "competence" to name occupational competence (Boam & Sparrow, 1992; Hendry, Arthur, & Jones, 1995). For Winterton and co-workers, "competency captures skills and dispositions beyond cognitive ability such as self-awareness, self-regulation and social skills". Winterton and co-workers conclude that "if intellectual capabilities are needed to develop knowledge and operationalizing knowledge is part of developing skills, all are prerequisites to developing competence, together with other social and attitudinal aspects". The statement they retain as being the clearest is from Woodruffe (1993) who defines "occupational competence" as "aspects of the job which an individual can perform, with competency referring to a person's behaviour and underpinning competent performance" where the competence-performance approach has been conceptualized in the line of Chomsky's work (1980) in linguistics.

More recently, Peregrin (2014) reminded us of guidelines provided by the American Northwestern University (2004): competencies may be seen as describing skills, knowledge and behaviour necessary to perform the job. In this case, skills would be abilities needed to execute job duties, such as software and computer proficiency, accounting skills or specific laboratory techniques (occupational competencies), and also interpersonal skills (generic competencies) (see also Heijke, Meng, & Ris, 2003). Knowledge would be linked with areas of specialty or expertise—for example, nursing, finance, employment law or history. Behaviour would be linked with characteristics an employee must display in the job—for instance, initiative, collegiality, resourcefulness or professionalism.

From the ex-Soviet researchers' standpoint, know-how refers to the knowledge of knowing how to do something and that knowledge may be considered as the combination of acquired data and acquired rules connected by the ability to manage them together (Ilyenkov, 2007) or, in other words, supported by the intellect (Leontiev & Luria, 2005 [1937]; Sokolova, 2012). Leontiev and Luria (2005 [1937]) suggest that skills are cognitive processes. These cognitive processes provide the link between acquired knowledge and what will later become competencies; acquired knowledge must first be transformed into know-how. Ilyenkov (2007) emphasizes this point as follows: "there must be a special ability that is distinct from knowledge itself, the ability to 'apply' the knowledge in one's possession". Considering this finding, Ilyenkov points out the necessary existence of a mediator between knowledge and competence, the "ability to apply" which he calls a "special skill": "the question arises: can this special skill be learned and taught?" Based on the "Critique of Pure Reason" by Kant, Ilyenkov demonstrated that this skill is an "innate ability". Before Ilyenkov, Talyzina (1984) highlighted how actions were necessary to achieve the learning process: "Actions thus are one of the components that determine the effectiveness of any learning process". We may extend her proposal to the previous considerations and suggest that actions contribute towards elaborating know-how from knowledge. Therefore, competencies coming through actions can only be achieved during an activity situation, determined by intentions, goals and context according to the Activity Theory (Leontiev, 1974; Nardi, 1995). Furthermore, competencies originating from knowledge, knowledge being specific and needing specific skills to rise in competencies, competencies are necessarily themselves specialized.

The French-speaking movements of ergonomics and psycho-sociology complement these findings with a lexical difficulty induced by the fact that "skills" and "competencies" are translated by the same French word "*compétences*". Montmollin (1986: 122) suggested a description of skills or competencies as "stabilized sets of knowledge and know-how, of typical behaviours, of standard procedures, of types of reasoning that one can implement without new training. Competencies [skills] stabilize and structure the achievements of professional history; they allow the anticipation of phenomena, of implicit within requirements, of variability in the task". For Samurçay (2005), a novice's anticipation is local, short loop while experienced workers have an overall anticipation of the system and are able to manage interactions between different phenomena. This means that novices have a superficial knowledge while experienced workers have a deeper understanding of the work situation. Leplat (2001) noticed that skills or competencies are unobservable by nature: only their manifestations may be observed.

In addition, some knowledge mobilized in work activity is experience based or "experiential" (learning is achieved through own experience and involvement), in most cases internalized as tacit knowledge (Polanyi, 1967). They have progressively become unconscious and may become automatisms (Nonaka & Takeuchi, 1995). The more experienced the worker, the more it becomes difficult to obtain the description of some actions of the work activity. The model developed by Nonaka (1991) distinguishes four knowledge conversion processes: Socialization,

Externalization, Combination and Internalization. It is the SECI model. "Socialization" allows the passage of tacit to explicit to promote transmission from the experienced worker to the novice. "Socialization" enables the sharing of experience and mental models; it is the case through mentoring. Yet as we explained, the process tends to diminish then disappear. "Externalization" is mostly verbal or written; this process is difficult to implement because tacit knowledge is necessarily difficult to verbalize. "Combination" is to combine discrete parts of explicit knowledge into a new whole. "Internalization" happens when new explicit knowledge is shared between workers through organization making some of them reframe their own tacit knowledge.

As can be seen, if all different schools of thought mention knowledge, know-how, skills and competencies and identify a link between them, the relationships remain slightly different from one to another and this diversity does not simplify the problem. Table 2.1 summarizes the results obtained through the literature review.

Therefore, an attempt to reconcile the considerations exposed in the literature review is needed. It cannot claim to be the truth but at least the most adapted choice to understanding the present issue. It gave the following.

Skills are consecutive to knowledge and know-how: knowledge is a prerequisite to skills since, before developing skills in a field, one must learn from oneself through heuristics or from others through lessons, imitation, training and so on. Know-how is also a prerequisite to skills in that it constitutes a lower level in terms of performance, of having the skills to perform a task. Know-how and skills develop through action: this refers to the ability to apply knowledge involving one or more cognitive processes. Action is resolutely necessary to transform knowledge into know-how which then becomes skill. These skills are also developed through action in situation: they are specialized. The action is therefore required to achieve the learning process if the outcome is the elaboration of know-how and skills.

There is thus a bilateral relationship which makes it impossible to dissociate action and skills: within the learning or working situation, competencies exist through action, and action in situation must necessarily produce competencies. This means that knowledge gives know-how through action and that know-how becomes skill through experience, that is the repetition of the subject's exposure in situations of action while having to apply knowledge and know-how. The repetition of the

Table 2.1 Definitions of knowledge, know-how, skills and competencies

Knowledge	*Know-how*	*Skills*	*Competencies*
• May concern a cognitive dimension and/or a behavioural dimension (Garvin, 1993) • Within a social system may have an organizational dimension (Senge, 1990). • Includes both declarative and tacit aspects resulting mainly from the experience (Eraut, 2000; Polanyi, 1958, 1967; Polanyi & Sen, 2009; Wagner & Sternberg, 1986) • Communities of practice are a necessary condition for tacit knowledge sustainability (Wenger, 1998) • Is prerequisite to developing competence (Winterton et al., 2006) • Combines acquired data and acquired rules linked by the ability to manage them together (Ilyenkov, 2007) • Is supported by the intellect (Leontiev & Luria, 2005 [1937]; Sokolova, 2012) • Is superficial for novices (Samurçay, 2005) • May be tacit or explicit (Polanyi, 1967) • Socialization allows the passage of tacit to explicit (Nonaka, 1991)	• Refers to the knowledge of how to do (Ilyenkov, 2007) • Is transformed from knowledge (Leontiev & Luria, 2005 [1937]) • Is elaborated from the knowledge through actions Talyzina (1984)	• Are goal-directed, well-organized behaviours that are acquired through practice and performed with economy of effort (Proctor & Dutta, 1995) • Have several dimensions: perceptual skills, response selection skills, motor skills and problem-solving skills (Proctor & Dutta, 1995) • Are highly integrated patterns of behaviour during acts following intention without conscious control (Rasmussen, 1983) • Occupational competencies: abilities needed to execute job duties (Peregrin, 2014) • Generic competencies: interpersonal skills (Heijke et al., 2003; Peregrin, 2014) • Are cognitive processes making link between the acquired knowledge and what will later become the competencies (Leontiev & Luria, 2005 [1937]) • Includes an innate ability to "apply" the knowledge (Ilyenkov, 2007) • Are unobservable by nature (Leplat, 2001)	• Capture skills and dispositions beyond cognitive ability such as self-awareness, self-regulation and social skills (Winterton et al., 2006) • Aspects of the job which an individual can perform, with competency referring to a person's behaviour and underpinning competent performance (Woodruffe, 1993) • Are the skills, knowledge and behaviour necessary to perform the job (Peregrin, 2014) • Are stabilized sets of knowledge and know-how, of typical behaviours, of standard procedures, of types of reasoning that one can implement without new training (Montmollin, 1986) • Are unobservable by nature (Leplat, 2001)

subject's exposure in a situation implies variability: experience develops through the variability of situations encountered (Montmollin, 1986; Rogalski & Leplat, 2011) since activities associated with a given task are always different due to changes in context, different interactions with co-workers and unplanned disturbances (Norros, 2004).

Analysis of work activities we already carried out in numerous situations in aircraft, medical and nuclear industries (Fauquet-Alekhine, 2011, 2012a, 2012b, 2012c, 2013, 2014; Fauquet-Alekhine, Berton, Rouillac, Geeraerts, & Granry, 2015; Fauquet-Alekhine & Boucherand, 2012; Fauquet-Alekhine, Geeraerst, & Rouillac, 2011; Fauquet-Alekhine & Labrucherie, 2008, 2012) showed that we may adopt a proposal that matches most of the considerations developed in the theoretical review above. It would be fastidious and without interest to give an example for each of the points in Table 2.1 and for each industry to demonstrate this; however, from a general standpoint, the aircraft pilots, the anaesthetists or the surgeons, the nuclear reactor pilots or their technician co-workers, all have shown acquiring new knowledge before developing new know-how.

The approach is thus to consider competencies as an overall concept designating knowledge, know-how and skills where knowledge is a prerequisite to know-how and skills. Skills develop from know-how in action with experience, where "experience" means being exposed to situations several times and at a certain frequency (it is quite different to perform a task once every ten years or ten times in one year). Having skills is therefore possessing know-how that has been put into action several times (in the event of the situation). Thus, identifying know-how and skills on paper may be difficult. Figure 2.1 summarizes the proposal in a concise schema highlighting the logical relationship between knowledge, know-how and skill, the whole being competencies. Competencies gain in efficiency when the subjects' number of exposures (Y-axis) to the situation increases and when its rate (X-axis) increases too. It also provides clear identification of the kinetics of loss of competencies (when the rate decreases) and conversely the kinetics of recovery of competencies. The triangular zone noted as an "inaccessible zone" is an arbitrary area postulated inaccessible as at least two exposures to a situation are needed to calculate a rate of exposure.

For the sake of accuracy below, we shall designate representation in Fig. 2.1 as the KKHS model (Knowledge, Know-How and Skills model).

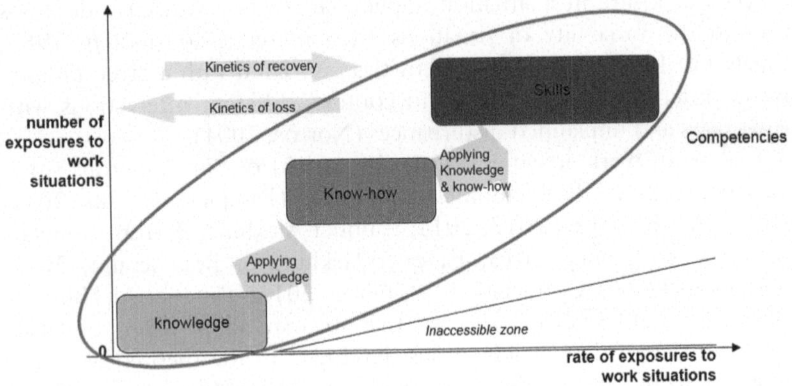

Fig. 2.1 Nesting concept of competencies based on knowledge, know-how and skills: the KKHS model

The KKHS model approach is consistent with the Knowledge Management paradigm. In their review addressing this issue, Alavi and Leidner (2001) suggested that knowledge may be viewed as a state of mind, an object (data, information), a process, an access to information or a capability. If we consider knowledge as a capability based on objects (data, information), it means that knowledge must be viewed first as a capability of knowing and understanding these objects (state of mind and access to information). All the concepts are linked except that of "process". The concept of process, referring to applying expertise (according to the authors), is set aside here because expertise refers to know-how rather than knowledge. In this case, "the view of knowledge as a capability suggests a knowledge management perspective centred on building core competencies, understanding the strategic advantage of know-how, and creating intellectual capital" (Alavi & Leidner, 2001: 10). In this perspective, the KKHS model helps to describe the process of creating and keeping competencies which is the first step of Knowledge Management defined as "the process of creating, sharing, using and managing the knowledge and information of an organization"; this is a universal definition of Knowledge Management according to the analysis undertaken by Girard and Girard (2015) in 23 different domains. However, if the KKHS model describes the process of creating and keeping competencies, it does not explain how to do it. For this aim, another model is needed, as we shall see in Chapter 3.

2.2 The KKHS Model Robustness

The KKHS model for Knowledge, Know-How and Skills could be described with the following intrinsic properties first formulated as hypotheses to be validated:

P1 The more the subject perceives him/herself competent/skilled, the more probable the competencies are associated by the subject with know-how or skills rather than knowledge.
P2 Knowledge is perceived as the basis of competencies.
P3 Competencies improvement is related to both the number of exposures to the activity and the frequency of exposures.

Let us remind here that knowledge and know-how are understood here according to the conclusions given in the previous section, as part of an overall concept of "competencies" designating knowledge, know-how and skills where knowledge is a prerequisite to know-how and skills.

To assess the validity of these properties (P1 to P3) and thus the operational validity of the model, they were tested by confronting workers' perceptions when putting their competencies in action for one of their work activities.

Subjects were individually contacted to assess statement S1 and answer questions Q1 and Q2[1]:

S1 In your opinion, you are skilled in this activity.
Q1 In your opinion, what is firstly required in terms of competencies for a novice who will perform this activity?
Q2 In your opinion, when performing this activity, do repetition or frequency most improve your skills?

S1 was a filtering statement in accepting or rejecting the subjects' contribution: as subjects were expected to describe their knowledge,

[1] In French, original questions were:

S1: Selon vous, vous êtes compétent pour cette activité.

Q1: Selon vous, qu'est-ce qui est d'abord requis pour un novice en termes de compétences pour réaliser cette activité?

Q2: Selon vous, réalisant cette activité, qu'est-ce qui améliore votre compétence entre la répétition et la fréquence?

know-how or skills, if they did not feel skilled in the activity they described, we might assume that it would be difficult for them to talk about their skills and thus create a bias in the data; these subjects would be rejected. Subjects' assessment for S1 was formed on a Likert scale (strongly disagree, disagree, neither disagree nor agree, agree, strongly agree) and the expected answer was "agree" or "strongly agree". In case of "neither disagree nor agree", a discussion was started to understand this choice and state whether the subject had to be rejected or not. The other answers led to reject the subject.

Q1 and Q2 were elaborated from the literature review with the objective of testing the operational validity of the model. Q1 was assumed to contribute to discriminate knowledge, know-how and skills and what was first required among them in a learning process. Q2 was formed so as to test the validity of the two dimensions of the model, the rate X-axis and the number Y-axis on Fig. 2.1.

Socio-demographic data was also collected. Data was used after statistical analysis.

$N=50$ subjects working at a French nuclear power plant (NPP) were contacted in 2017. They all had different professions and different positions. This ensured that each of the 50 cases referred to different activities: all 50 cases could be taken into account within the sample without causing any redundancy bias. They were chosen at random among the 300 professions and the 1200 employees at the NPP. For example, some of the professions and activities were surface cleaning technician for the activity "emptying all the trashcans of the offices of the building", safety expert for the activity "daily unit safety check-up" and operating reactor pilot for the activity "control room safety check-up".

The average age was 37.8 years ($SD=9.3$) and average professional experience was 6.4 years ($SD=6.7$), with a 72% male population (a high proportion due to the preponderance of physically demanding and operational jobs at the plant as well as the small number of tertiary jobs usually occupied by women. Plant history also played a role in the preponderance of men working at the plant).

The profession sample grouped 40% management positions and 20% tertiary professions, the remaining participants being technicians or engineers in operational or maintenance departments. At the NPP, the proportion of managers and tertiary positions was slightly different: 25% of staff had managerial positions and 20% were tertiary. The difference in the number of management positions could be reduced by increasing the number of subjects (but it might have created a bias by integrating similar professions within the sample) or decreasing the number of participants which was not desired. The aim was to test the KKHS model; thus, the need was not to obtain a representative sample of the NPP population but to undertake a test with a wide range of professions.

The results obtained were a shortened formulation of the subjects' answers, the expression of which was validated by the subjects during the interviews. The results were taken down by the analyst during the interviews and then collected for statistical analysis.

For ethical reasons, the detailed results could not be included in the present book: some professions being unique, the persons having participated in the survey would have been easily recognized by colleagues when reading the book. Ethical approval (Code of Approval: DSP/RS/PFA-4) for the study was obtained from the Ethics Committee of the Department of Social Psychology (LSE, London, UK).

The mean score for S1 ("In your opinion, you are skilled in this activity") was 1.34 on a Likert scale coded from −2 (strongly disagree) to +2(strongly agree), showing that subjects agreed or strongly agreed with the fact that they felt competent/skilful to perform the activity they chose to describe. All individual scores were 1 or 2 except for three of them who scored 0 (neither agree nor disagree):

- Two of these scores referred to a situation for which managers are not trained, for which knowing how to manage the situation comes from individual experience (no mentoring) and for which there is no clear assessment of success in terms of results; for example, "dealing with an interpersonal conflict in the team" may be perceived as a success if the conflict is solved; however, the situation has been managed.
- One of these scores referred to a subject periodically confronted with situations exposing the subject to others while handing in the results of his/her work.

However, these subjects were not rejected from the sample as we were addressing the existence of knowledge and know-how, not the fact that subjects might or might not be formally trained within the professionalization strategy of the company.

Regarding Q1 ("In your opinion, what is firstly required in terms of competencies for a novice who will perform this activity?"), 64%

answered details referring to knowledge, 34% to know-how and for these, the description they gave showed that this know-how was underpinned by knowledge. This allowed us to validate P2 (knowledge is perceived as the basis of competencies).

Considering subjects referring first to knowledge on the one hand and know-how on the other when answering Q1, we tried to identify features characterizing these two groups.

Nothing could be found from average values of independent variables:

- The average age for each group was resp. 37.9 and 37.8 not significantly differing (t-test: $t(df=47)=0.12$; $p>0.9$).
- The average experience for each group was resp. 6.6 and 6.3 not significantly differing (t-test: $t(df=47)=0.39$; $p>0.7$).
- The average score regarding competencies perception for each group was resp. 1.4 and 1.3 not significantly differing (t-test: $t(df=47)=0.50$; $p>0.6$).

However, when considering modal distributions, conclusions were quite different.

- The modal distribution regarding age for each group significantly differed according to χ^2-test ($\chi^2(1,fd=4)=15.03$; $p<0.0001$): know-how was answered preferentially by older workers.
- The modal distribution regarding experience for each group significantly differed according to χ^2-test ($\chi^2(1,fd=3)=8.55$; $p<0.04$): know-how was answered preferentially by experienced workers.

These results allowed us to state the following finding: the more workers are experienced (often related to older age) the more they think competencies first in terms of know-how (KH), while the less experienced they are (often related younger) the more they think competencies first in terms of knowledge (K). If we postulate that experienced workers perceive themselves competent more readily than novices, then it comes to validate P1 (the more the subject perceives him/herself competent/skilled, the more probable the competencies are associated by the subject with know-how or skills rather than knowledge).

Regarding Q2 ("In your opinion, when performing this activity, do repetition or frequency most improve your skills?"), 84% answered that both repetitions of exposure to the situation and frequency made them improving their activity, 12% answered only repetition, and 0% chose only frequency. This allowed us to validate P3 (competencies improvement is related to ***both*** the number of exposure to the activity and the frequency of exposure). The group of 12% answering only repetition was characterized by a low experience (4.1y compared to 6.4y for the whole sample) and a management position (66% of managers).

The overall results allowed us to validate the KKHS model.

To conclude this chapter, the Knowledge–Know-How–Skills model (KKHS model) depicts competencies as an overall concept designating knowledge, know-how and skills in the paradigm of Knowledge Management and shows that knowledge is a prerequisite to know-how and skills. Skills develop from know-how in action with experience, where "experience" means being exposed to situations several times and at a certain frequency. Having skills is therefore possessing know-how that has been put into action several times in the situation. The KKHS model also illustrates how know-how and skills are grounded in knowledge.

References

Alavi, M., & Leidner, D. E. (2001). Knowledge management and knowledge management systems: Conceptual foundations and research issues. *MIS Quarterly, 25,* 107–136.

American Northwestern University. (2004). *Guidelines for writing a competency based job description* (Report). http://www.northwestern.edu/hr/compensation/GuidelinesCompetencybasedJD.pdf.

Argyris, C., & Schön, D. A. (1974). *Theory in practice: Increasing professional effectiveness.* London: Jossey-Bass.

Argyris, C., & Schön, D. A. (1978). *Organisational learning.* Reading, MA: Addison-Wesley.

Bateson, G. (1973). *Steps to an ecology of mind.* New York: Ballantine Books.

Boam, R., & Sparrow, P. (1992). *Designing and achieving competency.* London: McGraw-Hill.

Boucher, X., Bonjour, E., & Grabot, B. (2007). Formalisation and use of competencies for industrial performance optimisation: A survey. *Computers in Industry, 58,* 98–117.

Chomsky, N. (1980). Rules and representations. *The Behavioural and Brain Sciences, 3,* 1–61.

Dodgson, M. (1993). Organisational learning: A review of some literature. *Organisational Studies, 14,* 375–394.

Eraut, M. (2000). Non-formal learning and tacit knowledge in professional work. *British Journal of Educational Psychology, 70,* 113–136.

Fauquet-Alekhine, Ph. (2011). Human or avatar: Psychological dimensions on full scope, hybrid, and virtual reality simulators. In *Proceedings of the Serious Games & Simulation Workshop* (pp. 22–36). Paris, France. http://hayka-kultura.org/larsen.html.

Fauquet-Alekhine, Ph. (2012a). Simulation training to prepare for robotic intervention in a hostile environment. *Socio-Organizational Factors for Safe Nuclear Operation, 1,* 88–93.

Fauquet-Alekhine, Ph. (2012b). Use of simulator training for the study of operational communication—The case of pilots of French nuclear reactors: Reinforcement of reliability. *Socio-Organizational Factors for Safe Nuclear Operation, 1,* 84–87.

Fauquet-Alekhine, Ph. (2012c). Safety and reliability for nuclear production. *Socio-Organizational Factors for Safe Nuclear Operation, 1,* 25–30.

Fauquet-Alekhine, Ph. (2013, August 15–16). Virtual training, human-computer & software interactions, and social-based embodiness. In *Proceedings of the International Conference on Electrical, Computer, Electronics and Communication Engineering* (pp. 364–370). Venice, Italy.

Fauquet-Alekhine, Ph. (2014). *Analyse organisationnelle & de besoins – Proposition de solutions: Volet Stratégique / Orientation Stratégique 1/4* [Organizational & needs analysis - Proposed solutions: Strategic segment / Strategic direction 1/4]. Analysis ref: DZ/./StratProf-analyse Besoins ind02.

Fauquet-Alekhine, Ph., Berton, J., Rouillac, L., Geeraerts, Th., & Granry, J. C. (2015). Systematic overestimation of perceived occupational stress. In *Proceeding of the 22nd International "Stress & Behavior" Conference—ISBC 2015* (p. 26). St Petersburg, Russia.

Fauquet-Alekhine, Ph, & Boucherand, A. (2012). The structuring effects of tools in risky industrial work activity: Failures and solutions. *Socio-Organizational Factors for Safe Nuclear Operation, 1,* 63–67.

Fauquet-Alekhine, Ph., Geeraerst, Th., & Rouillac, L. (2011). Cognitive disorder and professional development by training: Comparison of simulator sessions for anesthetists and for nuclear reactor pilots. In *Proceedings of the XVe European Conference on Developmental Psychology* (pp. 83–88). Pianoro (Italia): Medimond Srl.

Fauquet-Alekhine, Ph., & Labrucherie, M. (2008). Debriefing as an analysis of simulated situations: comparison between nuclear reactors operators and civil aircraft pilot. In *Proceedings of the Symposium Activity 2008—Activity Analyses for Developing Work* (p. 33). Helsinki, Finland.

Fauquet-Alekhine, Ph, & Labrucherie, M. (2012). Simulation training debriefing as a work activity analysis tool: The case of nuclear reactors pilots and civil aircraft pilots. *Socio-Organizational Factors for Safe Nuclear Operation, 1,* 79–83.

Garvin, D. (1993). Building a learning organization. *Harvard Business Review, 71*(4), 78–91.

Girard, J., & Girard, J. (2015). Defining knowledge management: Toward an applied compendium. *Online Journal of Applied Knowledge Management, 3*(1), 1–20.

Heijke, H., Meng, C., & Ris, C. (2003). Fitting to the job: The role of generic and vocational competencies in adjustment and performance. *Labour Economics, 10*(2), 215–229.

Hendry, C., Arthur, M. B., & Jones, A. M. (1995). *Strategy through people: Adaptation and learning in the small-medium enterprise*. London: Routledge.

Ilyenkov, E. V. (2007 [2002]). A Contribution on the question of the concept of "activity" and its significance for pedagogy. *Journal of Russian and East European Psychology, 45*(4), 69–74.

Leontiev, A. N. (1974). The problem of activity in psychology. *Soviet Psychology, 13*(2), 4–33.

Leontiev, A. N., & Luria, A. R. (2005 [1937]). The problem of the development of the intellect and learning in human psychology. *Journal of Russian and East European Psychology, 43*(4), 34–47.

Leplat, J. (2001). Compétence et ergonomie. In J. Leplat et M. Montmollin (Eds.), *Les compétences en ergonomie* (pp. 41–53) Paris: Octares.

Montmollin (de), M. (1986). *L'intelligence de la tâche: éléments d'ergonomie cognitive*. Berne: Peter Lang.

Nardi, B. (1995). Studying context: A comparison of activity theory, situated action models, and distributed cognition. In B. Nardi (Ed.), *Context and consciousness: Activity theory and human-computer interaction* (pp. 35–52). Cambridge: MIT.

Nonaka, I. (1991). The knowledge-creating company. *Harvard Business Review, 85*(7–8), 162–171.

Nonaka, I., & Takeuchi, H. (1995). *The knowledge-creating company*. Oxford: Oxford University Press.

Norros, L. (2004). *Acting under uncertainty: The core-task analysis in ecological study of work*. Espoo, Finland: VTT Publications.

Peregrin, T. (2014). Competency-based hiring: The key to recruiting and retaining successful employees. *Journal of the Academy of Nutrition and Dietetics, 114*(9), 1330–1339.

Polanyi, M. (1958). *Personal knowledge: Towards a post-critical philosophy*. London: Routledge & Kegan Paul.

Polanyi, M. (1967). *The tacit dimension*. New York: Anchor Books.

Polanyi, M., & Sen, A. (2009). *The tacit dimension*. Chicago, IL: University of Chicago Press.

Proctor, R. W., & Dutta, A. (1995). *Skill acquisition and human performance*. London: Sage.

Rasmussen, J. (1983). Skills, roles, and knowledge: Signals, signs, and symbols, and other distinctions in human performance models. *IEEE Transaction on Systems, Man, and Cybernetics SMC, 13*(3), 257–266.

Rogalski, J., & Leplat, J. (2011). L'expérience professionnelle: expériences sédimentées et expériences épisodiques. *Activités, 8*(2), 4–31. http://www.activites.org/v8n2/rogalski.pdf.

Samurçay, R. (2005). Concevoir des situations simulées pour la formation pour la formation professionnelle. In P. Pastré (Ed.), *Apprendre par la simulation – De l'analyse du travail aux apprentissages professionnels* (pp. 221–240). Octarès: Toulouse.

Senge, P. M. (1990). *The fifth discipline: The art and practice of the learning organization*. New York: Doubleday.

Sokolova, E. (2012). Does activity theory have a future? *Social Sciences, 1*, 85–97.

Talyzina, N. (1984). The contemporary condition of the activity theory of learning. *Contemporary Educational Psychology, 9*, 229–234.

Wagner, R. K., & Sternberg, R. J. (1986). Tacit knowledge and intelligence in the everyday world. In R. J. Sternberg & R. K. Wagner (Eds.), *Practical intelligence: Nature and origins of competence in the everyday world* (pp. 51–83). Cambridge: Cambridge University Press.

Wenger, E. (1998). *Communities of practice: Learning, meaning, and identity*. Cambridge, UK: Cambridge University Press.

Winterton, J., Delamare-Le Deist, Fr., & Stringfellow, E. (2006). *Typology of knowledge, skills and competences: Clarification of the concept and prototype* (Report of the European Centre for the Development of Vocational Training, Cedefop Reference Series: 64). Luxembourg: Office for Official Publications of the European Communities.

Woodruffe, C. (1993). *Assessment centres: Identifying and developing competence*. London: Institute of Personnel Management.

CHAPTER 3

Competencies Need Actions

Abstract This chapter examines theories and key concepts regarding competencies and activity, and emphasizes the importance of the notion of "competencies in action". It reviews the available models which might depict this concept. This results in developing a new model, the Square of PErceived ACtion model (SPEAC model) by adapting Le Boterf's model. A comparative analysis with existing models for competencies is provided on the basis of data analysis.

Keywords Competencies · Action · Activity Theory · Distributed Cognition · Square of PErceived ACtion model

3.1 Competencies and Workers

In the aim of considering "competencies in activities", we chose to review the Activity Theory and Distributed Cognition from the outset in order to provide key concepts to clarify this notion.

Activity Theory
Several approaches of Activity Theory exist in scientific literature which vary depending on the disciplinary standpoint of the authors.

Activity Theory originates from 1920s Soviet psychology and began to be disseminated internationally from the 1970s. Activity Theory

P. Fauquet-Alekhine, *Knowledge Management in High Risk Industries*, https://doi.org/10.1007/978-3-030-49213-7_3

then developed in the Soviet Union (Leontiev, 1974, 1975; Lomov, 1963; Rubinstein, 1922, 1935, 1940, 1946) and appeared as one of the essential sources of renewal and development of psychology and ergonomics. Increases in the number of Action Theory publications in Western Europe and Anglo-Saxon countries are proof of this: the number of translations of Russian authors increased, and works of syntheses appeared (Bedny & Meister, 2014; Bødker, 1989, 1991, 1996; Cole, 1998; Daniellou & Rabardel, 2005; Engeström, 1990; Kuutti, 1991, 1996; Kaptelinin 1996; Kaptelinin, Kuutti, & Bannon, 1995; Nardi, 1995; Nosulenko & Rabardel, 2007; Rabardel & Pastré, 2005). In 1962, the *International Journal of Psychology* was created in the USA, publishing the translated and original materials of predominant authors from countries of the former Soviet Union and Eastern Europe. The journal went under the names of *Soviet Psychology and Psychiatry* (1962–1966) and *Soviet Psychology* (1966–1991), and since January 1992 is known as the *Journal of Russian & East European Psychology* (6 issues per year).

Theories of activity provide methodological tools that facilitate the analysis of occupational activities in technological contexts. According to Barabanschikov (2007), the synthesis of the approaches of Russian psychology reveals a series of important properties of activity: there is no activity without subject and object, the activity is conscious, and it is social in nature.

Rubinstein, precursor of the theory, considered that studies in psychology should focus on the subject. He had therefore developed an anthropocentric approach towards activity: subject-oriented activity (Rubinstein, 1922). The strength of his theory lays in the fact that it permitted circumvention of the methodological opposition between "objective" and "subjective": consciousness and perceptions are subjective constructs that are an objective reality for the subject. The subjective exists objectively. It is thus observable and assessable either by objective measurements of the physiological state, or through the description that the subjects produce themselves about their internal states (thoughts, emotions, feelings). Around 1920, Rubinstein worked on the traditional opposition between consciousness and activity. His reflections on the question led to the unification of these two concepts by a new methodological principle, consciousness that manifests and develops itself in the activity: activity and consciousness are two potential intermediates of the interaction between the subject and the object of the subject's activity (the motive). This brought Rubinstein to the concept of subject-oriented activity.

Rubinstein then extended his work by considering the personality in the activity, associated with the concepts of consciousness, needs and capabilities. The unit consciousness-activity therefore implied considering the personality-activity unit (Aboulkhanova, 2007). The subject achieves lifelong unity of personality and of consciousness. Rubinstein's work led to a dynamic model of the personality-activity system (see Fig. 3.1). The dynamic character of the structure is particularly linked to the mobile nature of the link between motive and goal: for example, the goal may detach and attach to a result, thus generating new goals.

Lomov developed a relationship with the Activity Theory which is similar to that of Rubinstein. Lomov considered that human cognition could not be studied independently of communication processes. This consideration led him to think of human communication and activity as two distinctive but interdependent characteristics of the subject, laying the groundwork for what would be called operational communication (see in appendix the definition of "operational communication"). He built a methodological approach of a systemic nature in psychology whereby a given object of study should be considered from

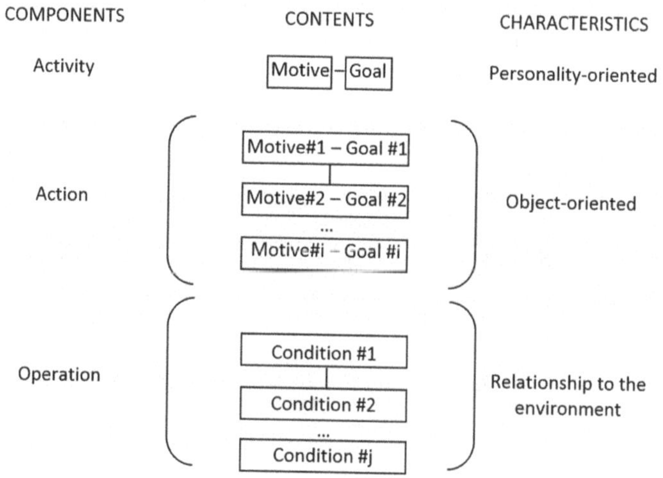

Fig. 3.1 Psychological structure of the activity according to Rubinstein (1946) (Adapted from Barabanchtchikov [2007])

various angles. In his book "Man and Technology" (Lomov, 1963), he advocated the need to take the human factor into account when designing tools and work systems. He thus suggested the bases of the psychology of engineering and contributed towards the foundations of the ergonomics of systems.

Leontiev, student of Vygotsky, developed a vision which was both bounded and exclusive of psychology, in that everything must be studied through activity and its structure. Despite the fact that, according to him, the Activity Theory was the only valid theory available to study human functioning, he focused only on individual activity. For Leontiev, the structure of the activity is determined by the object of activity, i.e. the motive (Fig. 3.2).

From a psychological standpoint, there are three dimensions of activity among which two are correlated. One is the observable external dimension (pink frame on Fig. 3.2) with the existence of structural units: activity, actions and operations. These units are the psychic reflection of the subject. The second dimension (purple frame on Fig. 3.2) is internal: it is the subordination of these structural units to the content of the object of activity: needs, motives, general and specific goals. Interaction of the subject with the object is an activity with regard to the motive and a set of actions with regard to the goal. In Leontiev's theory, the object of activity matches the motive of activity. This motive is an objectified need, from a need perceived as lacking. The motive carries

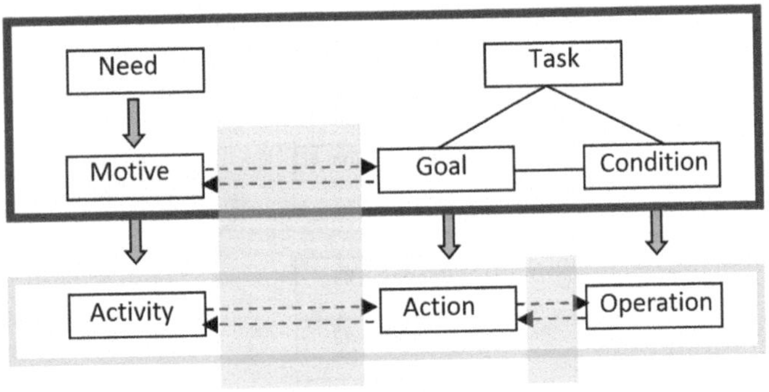

Fig. 3.2 Psychological structure of the activity according to Leontiev (1965) (Adapted from Barabanschikov [2007]: external dimension [pink frame], internal dimension [purple frame], relationship dimension [green area])

stimulation, since it satisfies a need. It is also the motor of activity: the motive boosts and guides the activity. The nature of this motive may vary and determines the form of the activity: a physical need leads to producing something tangible (physical object), a cognitive need leads to intellectual production (e.g. production of rules or instructions), and a functional need (e.g. maintaining one's physical condition) leads to functional activity (e.g. a sports activity). The goal is the conscious mental representation of the expected result. The goal is to the action what the motive is to the activity. It represents the object that guides the action. Tasks are associated with specific goals in context. Performing the activity is conditioned by the logic of the progress of the goals or tasks performance and is accomplished through actions subordinated to conscious goals. Operations correspond to the means of implementation of actions and are directly determined by the tasks. These components of activity cannot be isolated from each other. They constitute a system whose relationships enable transformations or shifts of components. The third relational dimension of activity (green area and dotted lines in Fig. 3.2) reflects the dynamic nature of activity. This flow of mutual transformations makes activity become action and conversely the action may become an activity; the motive can become a goal and vice versa. Similarly, when the action is more conscious, it becomes an operation and the operation may become action whenever a problem occurs and interrupts the automatic process implemented.

The goal-directed action theory (Von Cranach & Kalbermatten, 1982; Von Cranach, Mächler & Steiner, 1985) is an example. It provides precise vocabulary describing mental processes related to the activity. It is based on an interview with self-confrontation for reflexive analysis and is extremely useful to understand better the cognitive mechanisms: the subjects individually watch video recordings of their own practices and are invited to share their cognitive processes during the replay action.

Communities have developed around this framework. This is particularly the case in the field of the "Human - Computer Interaction", of which Susanne Bödker initiated the movement in the late 1980s (Bannon & Bødker, 1991; Bødker, 1989, 1991; Kaptelinin, 1996; Kaptelinin et al. 1995; Kaptelinin & Nardi, 1997; Kuutti, 1991, 1996; Nardi, 1996). This community of researchers showed how Activity Theory provides a framework for effective analysis to study the interactions between humans and artefacts that they manipulate, in their historical and cultural context.

Another community was born around (Engeström, 1990; Engeström & Middleton, 1996; Engeström, Miettinen, & Punamäki, 1999) regarded as one of West European specialists in the development of Activity Theory in the field of education science. Engeström suggested an enriched structure of the activity defined by Leontiev by adding the concepts of rule, community and division of labour. His first attempt modelled activity on Vygotsky's concept of mediation bringing together human actions and cultural artefacts but this model presented the drawback to focus on the subject. He thus suggested that mediation should be considered according to its relationship with other components of an activity system as artefacts had to be seen "as integral and inseparable components of human functioning" (Engeström et al., 1999: 29). The activity was considered at a macro-level: introducing the community, he integrated social collective elements in the activity system organized through rules and implying division of labour, all of them interacting through relationships schematized in its model by two nested triangles (Fig. 3.3): "Within the community, the members continuously negotiate their division of labour, including the distribution of rewards. The temporal rhythms of work, the uses of resources, and the codes of conduct are also continuously constructed and contested in the form of explicit and implicit rules" (Engeström, 2006: 4). The system was seen as producing object-oriented actions characterized by sense, the outcome

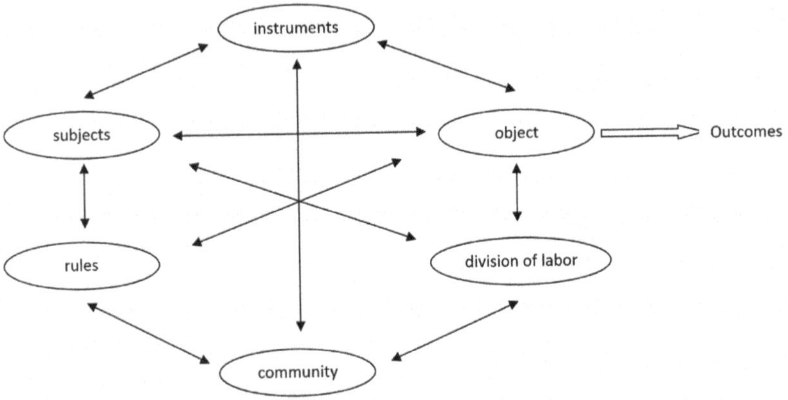

Fig. 3.3 Engestrom's activity system (Adapted from Engestrom, 2006)

being elaborated through multiple transformations from the original idea to the finished and stabilized object.

Joint activities could therefore be easily modelled by two activity systems interconnected through a shared object defined as a "potential common ground or synergy between the two [system] perspectives" (Engestrom, 2006: 4). Within such a network of activity, Engestrom emphasized the importance of contradictions and constraints in the definition of the motives and the object of the activity. According to Engestrom et al. (1999), activity had to be considered as a system within its network relations to other activity systems (underlining the importance of the relationship of the activity to other activities), each of them taken as the prime unit of analysis.

In France, the work of Ombredane and Faverge (1955) can be considered as a parallel current to the Soviet developments of the time. They proposed a conceptual framework similar to that provided by the Russian theories of activity. Other French researchers used the Activity Theory as a conceptual framework (Clot, 1999, 2001; Rabardel & Pastré, 2005; Rogalski & Samurçay, 1993).

Distributed Cognition

Facing the analysis of collaborative activities in the present study, the Distributed Cognition approach is essential. In this approach, the unit of analysis is a cognitive system composed of individuals and artefacts they use (Flor & Hutchins, 1991; Heath & Luff, 1991; Rogers & Ellis, 1994). This approach provides a framework for a detailed analysis of the artefacts, provides widely applicable design axes and studies the interactions between humans and the system and the human-human interaction, i.e. the phenomenon of coordination or collaboration. The strength of this approach lies in its interest in the phenomena of coordination/cooperation which operate within the groups.

Derived from cybernetic theories (Ashby, 1957; Wiener, 1948) and from the general theory of systems (Von Bertalanffy, 1968), Distributed Cognition is an approach that focuses on the functioning of the system. It seeks not only to emphasize the internal representations of the subject but is also interested in the representations created and disseminated through the artefacts, to provide a detailed analysis of these (Hutchins, 1995a; Nardi, 1996; Norman, 1991) to identify ultimately the broad principles of design that are widely applicable.

Numerous studies were conducted to examine the way several individuals coordinate while performing tasks on a system and sharing a common goal of production or realization: ship navigation (Hutchins, 1995a), aircraft flight in cockpit (Hutchins, 1995b, Hutchins & Klausen, 1996), engineering practices (Rogers, 1993) and computer specialists working in teams (Flor & Hutchins, 1991). These studies highlighted the crucial role of objects (cognitive artefacts, mediation structures) in the coordination and performance of the action.

Distributed Cognition (Hutchins & Klausen, 1996; Rogers & Ellis, 1994) considers the coordination techniques of subjects sharing a common goal within functional systems, i.e. individuals and artefacts and their relations to each other while performing a given task. As Situated Activity, Distributed Cognition points out the necessity of coordination for successful collaboration and therefore the necessity of existing factors of coordination (e.g. interfaces, communications). As for Activity Theory, Distributed Cognition emphasizes the importance of the goal of the activity and highlights the necessity for this goal to be shared by co-workers in order to obtain collaboration: co-workers elaborate shared expectations giving rise to a shared goal. As pointed out by Zager (2002), this means that if interaction or collective objects (including activity goal) do not exist, collaboration does not occur. Yet Distributed Cognition suggests a broader scope of analysis for socio-technical systems: the central unit of analysis being the functional system, it analyses how the content of this system is physically distributed (over artefacts related to users), socially distributed (through representations among subjects) and temporally distributed with the propagation of knowledge and information through the system (dynamic aspect) (Kirsh, 2000). This distribution-based approach permits the mapping out of the shared knowledge and associated communication vectors at both individual and collective levels. It may show complementary and redundant knowledge between co-workers, mismatches between shared expectations, or knowledge propagation disruptions causing coordination disturbance and therefore limiting the possible performance for the collaborative activity.

Activity Theory vs Distributed Cognition

Halverson (2002) undertook a comparative analysis between Activity Theory (AT) and Distributed Cognition (DCog) applied in the field of Computer Supported Cooperative Work. Despite several common points (both include the social and cultural context of cognition, both share a commitment to ethnographically collected data), she pointed out that "Although a DCog analysis is centred on cognitive processing, AT keeps process explicitly in the foreground by diagramming relations between elements within the activity system" which is very useful to identify "various elements and their relationships to explain the workings of the system" (p. 260). In addition, "AT's basic structure posits certain kinds of process interrelationships, which are implicit even when the analyst may not make them explicit. DCog obscures those relationships somewhat by focusing on the lower level" (p. 261). Furthermore, several authors recommend AT for studying collaborative activities. According to Antoniadou (2011), many studies have highlighted how AT could help in understanding the complexity of collaborative activities towards the achievement of a shared object by means of various artefacts. More recently, Stuart (2014) showed how Activity Theory was an appropriate frame for professionals seeking to understand how to work collaboratively which was already suggested earlier by Bardram (1998): "Activity Theory seems to provide appropriate conceptualizations, suited for analysing cooperative work its dynamic transformation, and the importance of cooperative breakdowns" (p. 91).

It is clear at this point that competencies must be mobilized in order to perform an activity and that this mobilization is multi-factorial and occurs when in action. Both AT and DCog, with their specificities and limits, may help to understand this process for which a model is needed.

3.2 Seeking Models for Competencies in Action

When searching a model linking competencies or skills and action inside the activity in the literature, one approach consists in looking for models of action and another one for model of competencies. Surprisingly, very few models are available in the literature from both sides.

Regarding models of actions, the model of Searle (2001) is derived from the model of Davidson (1980), the latter being called the "classical model" by Searle. Briefly, both are based on the subject's desire and belief to draw and trigger the action with a rational dimension that is mainly a matter of rules in the classic model. Searle added the notions of rationality related to free will before action and adjustment during action. Free will explains the gap between the motivation desire and the decision-making. Searle also emphasized the importance of a "motivator" for action which may be internal (a desire) or external (an obligation). While the models focus on the articulations between rationality, motives and action, none of them consider competencies related to action.

Gollwitzer (1990) suggested a model of "action phases" with four different consecutive action phases of goal pursuit: the predecisional phase for deliberation regarding desirability and feasibility of goals, the preactional phase to determine means and time to act towards the chosen goal, the actional phase implying a series of goal-directed behaviour towards achieving the goal and the postactional phase for assessment of the achieved outcomes (Faude-Koivisto, Wuerz, & Gollwitzer, 2009; Gollwitzer, 1990; Heckhausen, 1991). The model was later refined and led to the mindset theory of action phases (see, for example, Gollwitzer, 2012) suggesting that when involved in the consecutive phases, some ways of thinking become prominent. The deliberative mindset relates to decision-making in the predecisional phase, and the implemental mindset in the preactional phase relates to planning the steps to reach the goal. The model suggests a comprehensive temporal perspective on the course of action and does not make link with competencies; it mainly deals with goal intentions and implementation intentions.

The models of situated action (de Fornel & Quéré, 1999; Suchman, 1987; Suchman and Trigg, 1991, 1993) present action as responses to the environment and related goals as retrofitting constructions of the subject compared to the activity carried out. In this context, the subject does not develop the goals of the action. The action itself is therefore a reaction to the situation experienced rather than an action in a situation. A first issue emerges here: action as reaction posits motives and goals at a secondary level when compared with the situation and suggests that there is no pre-existing knowledge to action as action develops only in situation. Moreover, these approaches focus on the situation and on the activity in a situation without paying enough attention to the subjects and their interpersonal relations, the artefacts and their interactions with subjects. These models can hardly fit the theoretical framework chosen for the present work, the Activity Theory (Leontiev, 1974; Nardi, 1995) within which we consider competencies coming through actions and being achieved within an activity situation, determined by intentions, goals and context.

The TOTE model suggested by Miller, Galanter, and Pribram (1960) was innovative in that the authors were first modelling the contribution of mediating vectors between stimulus and response in action. They described action as successive steps and feedback within a progressive structure: Test–Operate–Test–Exit. However, the action is restricted to a simple and limitative cognitive process which does not relate to competencies and remains far from the notion of activity.

The model of planned action (Ajzen, 1985; Fishbein & Ajzen, 1975) introducing the cognitive intentional dimension of action models the relationships between beliefs, attitudes, behavioural intentions and behaviour: behavioural intentions and behaviour are shaped by subjective norms, perceived behavioural control and attitudes towards the behaviour itself. Like the TOTE model, the model of planned action is mainly cognitive processing based as a linear decision-making process: it does sufficiently account for factors influencing intentions and motivations such as emotions and past experiences. It focuses on beliefs and attitudes, without consideration for competencies needed to achieve the goals.

Regarding general models of skills or competencies (as opposed to specific skills or competencies models dealing, for example, with reading or leadership), the well-known Dreyfus's skills model (Dreyfus & Dreyfus, 1980) is limited to a suggestion of different steps characterizing the subject's levels of competencies; the model slightly changed after the original version and Eraut (2000) suggested: novice (rigid compliance with rules mainly), advanced beginner (actions based on attribute or aspects), competent (have developed know-how with experience), proficient (develop their own rules and their repertoire of experienced situations) and expert/master (choose intuitively the appropriate action from their repertoire of experienced situations, characterized by an unconscious fluid performance). Introducing intuition at the expert/master level, Dreyfus and Dreyfus supposed a progression from rigid compliance to rules to intuitive reasoning based on tacit knowledge (even though their original paper did not mention "tacit"). However, the model promotes intuition at the expense of analytical thinking (see, for example, Gobet & Chassy, 2009) and does not provide any explicit link to action.

The revised Bloom's taxonomy (Bloom, Engelhart, Furst, Hill, & Krathwohl, 1956; Krathwohl, 2002), approaching skills and competencies according to a classification of learning objectives into three domains (cognitive, affective, psychomotor), makes a link with action by introducing action verbs (analysed in depth by many researchers; e.g. Ven & Chuang, 2005) related to each category. The model is adapted to align pedagogical objectives with tasks and assessments but it focuses on subjects' changes in behaviour whereas transformation is not addressed. Another limitation of the model might relate to the fact that categorizing cognitive processes into clearly differentiated classifications might undermine the holistic nature of cognition. However, the main issue of the model in association with the present concern (analysing work activities in complex socio-technical systems) is that this approach is devoted to a mental activity, remains far from the notion of activity and cannot thus easily address our concern.

The motor skills model of Argyle and Kendon (1967) was elaborated to explain social interactions considering that social skills operate much like a serial skills motor. The model assumes subjects' motivation is sustained by goals which are achieved through a systematic and progressive loop adjusted by a perceived (perceptive capacities) and integrated (translation) feedback in order to respond to the outcomes of previous actions. The model is graphically depicted in Fig. 3.4.

This model is interesting in that it considers competencies (central box of the graph) coming through actions (the feedback loop) and being achieved within an activity situation, determined by intentions and goals (left side of the graph) and context (right side of the graph). The weakness of this model lies in a lack of descriptive relationships between competencies and action incorporated into the words "translation" and "feedback".

The last model found in the literature is the one proposed by Le Boterf (1998) regarding competencies at work, explicitly associated

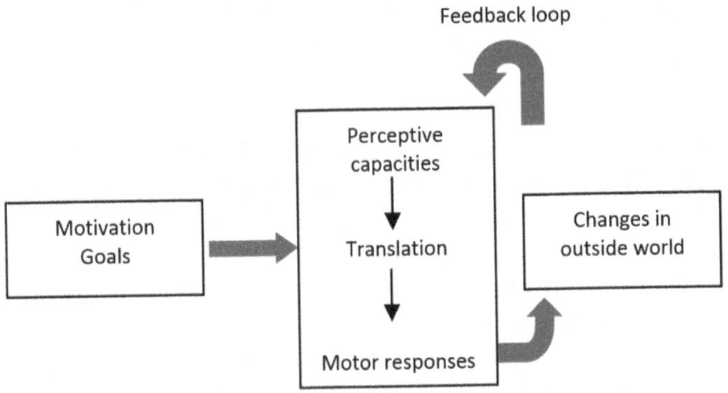

Fig. 3.4 Motor skills model (Adapted from Argyle and Kendon [1967])

with work activity. The model relates to action in the way Le Boterf depicted competencies at work involving action through the verb "to act", "*agir*" in French. He defined competencies as a system of three poles: in French, "Savoir agir", "Vouloir agir" and "Pouvoir agir". Valdes Conca and de Juana-Espinosa (2012: 234) as other authors referring to Le Boterf's French work, translated as the interaction of three poles: Knowing how to act, Wanting to act and Being able to act. This includes a mistake in the translation; the right meaning is: **Knowing to act, Wanting to act, Being able to act**. This point will be argued later.

Le Boterf's model defines thus competencies as an interacting system of three poles, drawing competencies as a triangle (Fig. 3.5). *Knowing to act* is that the professional will know to implement in situations, whether planned or unexpected provided that it is within the bounds of the profession; this is the practical implementation of the know-how, knowledge, all personal endogenous professional resources which combine themselves in knowing how to act in situations. *Wanting to act* refers to the motivation and the personal commitment of the professional. *Being able to act* reflects the context of the situation of work, the external, exogenous resources of the professional: material means and logistical resources, work organization and the social conditions that make it possible and legitimate responsibility and risk-taking of the professional. *Being able to act* is exogenous by the necessary means to act and therefore by the tools used which may be external to the subject (a hammer) or internal (a procedure known but not necessarily understood or simply the

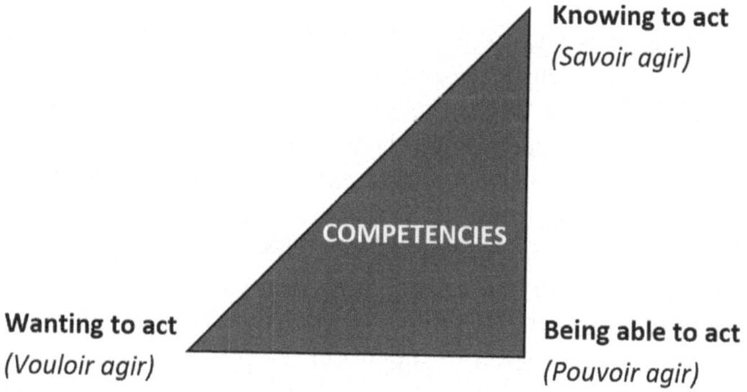

Fig. 3.5 Triangle of the competencies (Adapted from Le Boterf [1998])

psychological or physiological state). *Being able to act* is therefore also endogenous.

The model suggests that the analysis of competencies must question the three poles. Each question must use the verb which characterizes the pole and must address action. In French, questions which come naturally in mind are:

- *Qu'est-ce que vous savez faire?*
- *Qu'est-ce que vous pouvez faire?*
- *Qu'est-ce que vous voulez faire?*

In English, a word for word translation of the questions is:

- What do you know to do?
- What are you able to do?
- What do you want to do?

We must note here that the questions use "to do" and not "to act". Indeed, in French as well as in English, focusing the question on "to act" would not make sense as the verbs which characterize the poles have to be used:

Qu'est-ce que vous savez agir? /What do you know [how] to act?

Using "to do" in the questions may nevertheless be considered correct provided that, to questioning competencies and therefore, according to the model, questioning "to act", the questions address "doing" in "action". This is in total agreement with the definitions given by the dictionaries for "*agir*" and "to act". They are similar.

Larousse dictionary gives "agir: faire quelque chose, être en action".

Oxford dictionary gives "to act: do something, take action".

Another linguistic subtlety concerns the pole "*Savoir agir*", translated as "Knowing to act". The related question in French is "*Qu'est-ce que vous savez faire?*", neither "*Est-ce que vous savez comment faire?*" nor "*Comment savez-vous faire?*". The English question is thus "What do you know to do?" without using "how". This is why we suggest that the right translation of "*Savoir agir*" is not "Knowing how to do/act" but "Knowing to do/act" despite this is not strictly correct English.

Le Boterf's model therefore suggested the premise of the strong relationship between action and competencies through the verb "to act". We could go further by suggesting that Le Boterf's model is not a model of competencies, but a model of competencies in action. The link between competencies and action is mandatory in order to make competencies visible. According to the review analysis of Coulet (2013: 14), "competencies are manifest in the interaction of a subject (or a group) with a task in a given situation".

In fact, watching a professional sat on a chair and knowing this professional is an experienced and clever worker makes one think that this professional has competencies. In other words, it is not necessary to be involved in action to have competencies or to assume someone's competencies, but competencies are not seen here, just inferred; for the competencies to be seen, observed, it is necessary that the professional summons them within an activity through action.

Le Boterf's model thus appears to be more suitable for describing competencies in action, but the following shows this is not enough.

3.3 A Model for Competencies in Action: The SPEAC Model

Le Boterf's model suggests that competencies are mobilized through three poles, *Knowing to act, Wanting to act and Being able to act.* However, no experiment is available to validate this assumption; this remains to be done and was the purpose of the study described in the next section.

3.3.1 Le Boterf's Model for Competencies in Action

As concluded in the previous section, the literature review showed that Le Boterf's model (1998) was the one which presented the closest link between competencies and action. The three poles of the model Fig. 3.5 were considered in order to describe activities by workers. The details collected through individual interviews were then attributed to the model poles as far as was possible. For this data collection, the same subjects involved in testing the KKHS model (N = 50, different professions and different positions) were individually asked to describe an activity requiring their professional competencies. During these individual interviews, the analyst was looking for elements relating to each part of Le Boterf's model (acceptation of the model to describe competencies in action) as well as looking for elements that would be required for competencies in action but not described by the model (rejection of the model). At this stage, a full description of the activity was not needed: the objective of the interview was to attain details that fitted the poles and to focus on details that did not match any pole. The assumption was that characterization of the non-attributed details, should they exist, could help to adapt Le Boterf's model to depict competencies in action.

Le Boterf's model was tested in an overall approach so as to describe competencies in action. This was done with the sample of subjects interviewed when testing the KKHS model. Among all N=50 subjects, all of them gave spontaneously details fitting each of the three poles of Le Boterf's model. In addition, even though a full description of the activity was not expected, all participants gave several details not described by these three poles. These additional details were sorted into nine categories as shown in Fig. 3.6.

The most interesting property of the categorization resulting from this pre-test was that, whatever the category, it was related to the fact that subjects *had to do it*, or, in terms of Activity Theory, to the motive(s) of their action. Furthermore, only two categories were associated with internal motives with a very low score (right-hand side of Fig. 3.6): "affective relationship" and "excitement due to interest". All other categories referred to an external obligation: expectations or prescriptions of someone else (manager, client, regulator through organization, documents, rules and laws). This exhibits that a motive was necessary to mobilize competencies in action: mobilization of competencies in action needs to be trigged and the trigger relates to motives. When considering the categories of motives obtained, we may even find that motives precede willingness.

This finding thus helped us to determine that a pole was missing in Le Boterf's model to describe competencies in action: the pole **Having to act**.

Hence, instead of considering the triangle of competencies, we must consider the square of action of the subject, even more precisely the square of perceived action.

3.3.2 The SPEAC Model

In the Square of PErceived ACtion (Fig. 3.7) or SPEAC model, *Having to act* and *Knowing to act* poles are mainly shaped by the organization, thus exhibiting an exogenous dimension: the former is driven by the order (client, manager) and by the definition of the task; *Wanting to act*

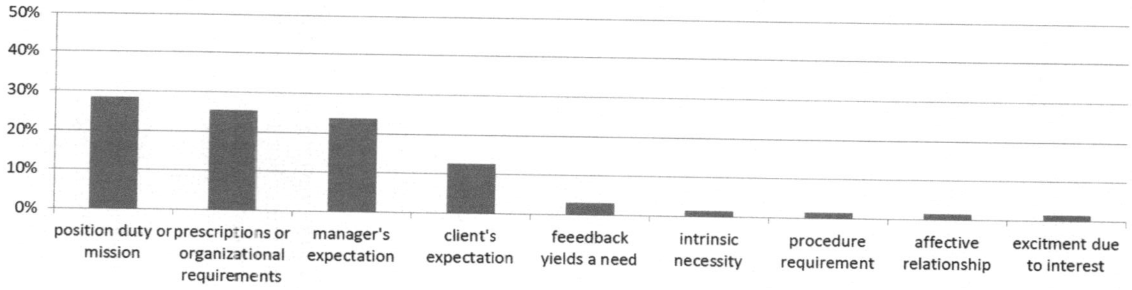

Fig. 3.6 Percentage per categories of details not described by Le Boterf's model three poles regarding $N=50$ subjects describing one of their activities for which they perceive themselves competent or skilful

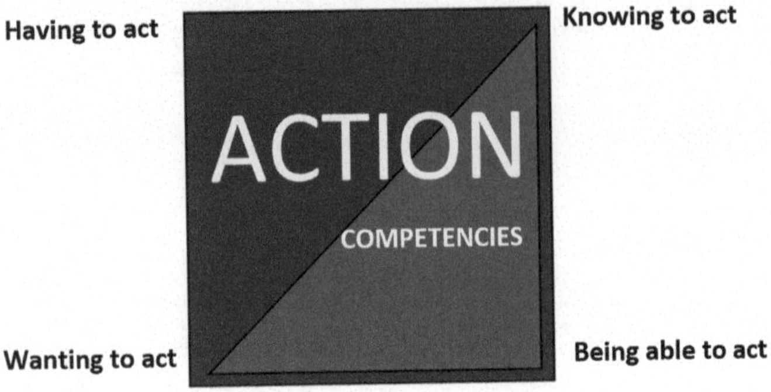

Fig. 3.7 Square of PErceived ACtion model (SPEAC model)

pole is mainly endogenous, decided by the subject, subjective; *Being able to act* is both endogenous and exogenous because related to the subject's capacities (subjective dimension) and to the means allocated to the activity (organizational dimension). Here *Being able to act* must be thought devoid of the notion of "being able to act because we know" as *Knowing to act* addresses this point. It is important to note that the gerundive form refers to a dynamic process, whereas organization, procedures and rules are static.

When a subject performs an activity, it is done by the means of actions, each having a goal. While the activity is led by a motive, action is directed by or towards a goal; it is goal oriented. For example, "hunger" is a motive (*Having to act*) that gives rise to the activity of feeding, and this activity may be composed of a set of actions. Different sets of actions can also be associated with the same activity. Feeding oneself by having a dinner at home does not involve the same actions that feeding by going to the fast-food restaurant. For this reason, a particular activity may be associated with different sets of goals, those guiding actions. One of the goals associated with having dinner at home may be to walk to the dining room; one of the goals of eating at fast-food restaurant may be to go out in the street to reach the fast-food restaurant. Each of these goals is different from the other and related to different actions. So far, the motive remains the same in both cases: "hunger". The action itself is broken down into operations (Fig. 3.2): the "going to the fast-food restaurant" action may presume to open the door of the apartment by moving the handle and pulling the door and then to close it, walk down the stairs, exit the building, walk ten minutes on the sidewalk,...

In addition, as the action is goal oriented, this assumes that there are one or more trajectories to achieve this goal. These trajectories correspond to the strategies deployed and therefore to what is implemented (a set of actions) to reach this goal. These trajectories are not frozen: the subject is usually able to adjust the path often to optimize energy expenditure according to the principle of cognitive economy (Allport, 1954; Kongovi, Guzman, & Dasigi, 2002). For example, "walk ten minutes on the sidewalk" may become "drive two minutes by car" (*Wanting to act*) because a friend drove by and proposed to drop the subject to the fast-food restaurant. The trajectory can be timed or adjourned. For example, the subject, once out of the building, reminds the need of cigarettes: the subject crosses the street to go to the tobacconist (*Wanting to act*), makes the purchase and goes back to the previous activity. These examples show that an activity may be accomplished by various actions but also that an action may be part of various activities, and therefore triggered by different motives (*Having to act*). Applying the Square of PErceived ACtion model (SPEAC model), *Having to act* is related to the motive "hunger" and to the goal "fast-food restaurant at the end of the trip". For this aim (reaching the goal), the subject must know to act and must be able to act. *Knowing to act* allows the subject to determine the set of operations that must be carried out taking into account what can be done, that is taking into account *Being able to act*. As the trajectory to reach the goal is not frozen, it may change while being performed. *Wanting to act* helps the trajectory to keep stable or change, as when the subject decides on the way to buy cigarettes or to take benefits of a friend's car. Similarly, *Being able to act* may lead the subject to adapt this trajectory: for example, meeting an obstacle on the way to the fast food such as men at work on the sidewalk, the subject will have to cross the street and use for a while another sidewalk than the one chosen at the beginning because of being the shorter way.

The SPEAC model can thus help us to explain the way trajectories to a goal may change by applying a pole-based protocol of analysis through the replay interview (Fauquet-Alekhine, 2016; Fauquet-Alekhine & Lahlou, 2017). To do so, we consider each pole of the SPEAC model and questions regarding both the positive and the negative aspect of the poles according to the Activity Theory perspective of "negative goal" as suggested by Lahlou (quoted by S. Le Bellu, 2011: 372). This relates to the necessity to take into account actions as well as non-action: "Non-actions are potential or possible actions not done but which might have been done, and are usually not observed" (Fauquet-Alekhine & Labrucherie, 2012: 79). Negative goals are related to the goals the subject does not want to reach; this approach is presented as new in that until then, the analyses of activities focused only on positive goals, the goals the subject wants to reach. Hence, the questions are basically as follows:

- Pole *Having to act* for the questions:
  What did you have to do? /What did you not have to do?
- Pole *Knowing to act* for the questions:
  What did you know how to do? /What did you not know how to do?
- Pole *Wanting to act* for the questions:
  What did you want to do? /What did you not want to do?
- Pole *Being able to act* for the questions:
  What were you able to do? /What were you not able to do?
  (in terms of means, not related to the knowledge).

As pointed out above, the two poles *Having to act* and *Knowing to act* are mainly defined by the organization before doing the activity: the worker knows usually what he/she has to do before performing the activity due to the prescription, the procedure related to the task and the manager's order, and he/she knows to do it because, as a professional identified to perform this task, he/she "obviously" had an occupational training for this purpose. The prescription, the manager's order and the professional training are for a great part defined before performing the activity through the task definition and the worker's official qualification.

These facts are considered independently from the actual degree of accuracy of the task definition and of the worker's official qualification. This means that these degrees of accuracy making *Knowing to act* are input data when investigating what makes workers' competencies and must be accepted as they are: the fact that a novice is judged by an experienced worker as someone not correctly prepared for the task but nevertheless said qualified by the management is an input data as well as the fact that an experienced worker may be an expert for the same task. Regarding *Having to act*, if it changes significantly, then it refers to another activity. For example, when *Having to act* is defined by a procedure, if the procedure changes significantly, the activity changes too.

On the contrary, the poles *Wanting to act* and *Being able to act* may be thought by the worker before performing the activity, but they may be continuously and significantly adjusted to the situation while performing the activity. These poles are less pre-defined by the organization than the two others.

Depending on the goal of the analysis, it is not injudicious to apply the model on the unique basis of the subjective description of the activity, even if it is incomplete. For example, since the model is presented as describing the necessary conditions for the subject to put successfully competencies in action, any weakness of the structure described by the model applied to an activity highlights and contributes to understand the problem encountered. To illustrate this, let us consider a manager asking an employee to provide a work of quality (part of *Having to act*), and at the same time, he limits the time allocated for this task (part of *Having to act*). If this time is too short to ensure the required quality of the work, these two parts of *Having to act* are not coherent: there are contradictory injunctions and thus competencies cannot be put successfully in action. This incoherence within the pole *Having to act* makes it difficult to put competencies successfully in action. Applying the model to this situation helps the analysts to characterize the psychological issue for the subject, here incoherence within the pole *Having to act*. It also helps the analysts to try to find a possible solution to this issue: Can the pole *Being able to act* provide a compensatory resource in terms of means, by providing more performing tools for instance? Incoherence within the pole *Having to act* refers to a static approach, and considering the interpolar relationship between *Having to act* and *Being able to act*, this refers to the dynamic approach and this short analysis is undertaken without the necessity to describing completely the activity or the competencies in action for this activity. In this case, the model is used as a tool that may provide a fast, objective and determinant identification of issues and associated remedial measures (see an example of application in Fauquet-Alekhine & Rouillac, 2016): indeed, the model can contribute to explaining why, in certain occupational contexts, workers may experience psychological difficulties or suffer from mental health issues.

To summarize about the static and dynamic approaches of the model, the static approach is to consider that "Putting competencies successfully in action" is obtained when the four poles are all effective. "Effective" means that the poles are both "available" and "coherent". "Available" means that the content of a pole is defined and actually exists for the subject to act. "Coherent" means that any part of a pole does not counteract another part of the same pole. Example: Having to act is not available if a procedure is missing and is not coherent if it is required to perform a job in less time than what is possible. The dynamic approach of the model considers the interpolar relationships; there are six within the square: the side relationships and the diagonal relationships. Each of them must give account for symmetrical adequacy between the poles. Any inadequacy between several poles may give rise to a conflict between these poles which may lead to difficulties for competencies to be successfully put in action. Example: *Having to act* and *Being able to act* are not in adequacy if you must write but there is no pen, no pencil. Hence, the dynamic approach (and thus the property of "adequacy") comes in addition to the static approach (properties of "availability" and "coherence"). Therefore, "Putting competencies successfully in action" is obtained when the four poles respect the properties of effectiveness and adequacy.

The comparative analysis between the SPEAC model and other models presented in the literature review is not very demanding as the weaknesses of these models regarding "describing competencies in action" are confirmed:

- The model of Davidson (1980) and the derived model of Searle (2001) do not consider competencies related to action, and its main weakness was its incapacity to take the means into account (all that the pole *Being able to act* describes).
- Gollwitzer's four "action phases" models (Faude-Koivisto et al., 2009; Gollwitzer, 1990; Heckhausen, 1991) proposing the predecisional phase, the preactional phase, the actional phase and the postactional phase do not make link with competencies; it mainly dealt with goal intention and implementation intention, i.e. focuses on the poles *Having to act* and *Wanting to act* and the associated relationship at the expense of knowledge and means.
- The situated action models (de Fornel & Quéré, 1999; Suchman, 1987; Suchman & Trigg, 1991, 1993) present action as responses to the environment and the related goals as retrofitting constructions of the subject compared to the activity carried out; in this context, the subject does not develop the goals of the action, a modelization that may work at the expense of what the pole *Having to act* represents.

- The TOTE (Test-Operate-Test-Exit) model suggested by Miller et al. (1960) considers the action is thus restricted to a limitative cognitive process which does not relate to competencies and remains far from the notion of activity; in particular, it cannot integrate most of the content of *Having to act* and *Being able to act*.
- The model of planned action (Ajzen, 1985; Fishbein & Ajzen, 1975) presents the same drawbacks as the TOTE model.
- The Dreyfus's skills model (Dreyfus & Dreyfus, 1980) does not propose any explicit link to action; this model appears as another way to depict elaboration of competencies; motives and means are hardly taken into account.
- The revised Bloom's taxonomy (Bloom et al., 1956; Krathwohl, 2002) is an approach devoted to a mental activity and remains far from the notion of activity, thus not adapted here.
- The motor skills model of Argyle and Kendon (1967) presents a major weakness relying on a lack of descriptive relationships between competencies and action incorporated into the words "translation" and "feedback", making the means rather not clearly integrated into the model; in addition, motives and willingness are considered as a unique entity of input data of the model which reduces the possibilities to analyse their interactions.

The SPEAC model is therefore a relevant and efficient tool to elaborate a protocol for work activity analysis aiming at identifying and accessing what makes workers' competencies and how to select what should be transferred.

References

Aboulkhanova, K. A. (2007). Le sujet de l'activité ou la théorie de l'activité selon SL Rubinstein. In P. Rabardel et V. Nosulenko (Eds.), *Rubinstein aujourd'hui. Nouvelles figures de l'activité humaine* (pp. 41–81). Paris: Octares et Maison des Sciences de l'Homme.

Ajzen, I. (1985). From intentions to actions: A theory of planned behavior. In J. Kuhl & J. Beckmann (Eds.), *Action control: From cognition to behavior* (pp. 11–39). Heidelberg, Germany: Springer.

Allport, G. W. (1954). *The nature of prejudice*. New York: Addison-Wesley.

Antoniadou, V. (2011). Using activity theory to understand the contradictions in an online transatlantic collaboration between student-teachers of English as a foreign language. *ReCALL, 23*(3), 233–251.

Argyle, M., & Kendon, A. (1967). The experimental analysis of social performance. *Advances in Experimental Social Psychology, 3*, 55–98.

Ashby, W. R. (1957). *An introduction to cybernetics*. London: Chapman & Hall Ltd.

Bannon, L., & Bödker, S. (1991). Beyond the interface: Encountering artefact in use. In J. Carroll (Ed.), *Designing interaction: Psychology at the human computer interface* (pp. 227–253). Cambridge: Cambridge University Press.

Barabanchtchikov, V. (2007). La question de l'activité dans la psychologie russe. In P. Rabardel et V. Nosulenko (Eds.), *Rubinstein aujourd'hui. Nouvelles figures de l'activité humaine* (pp. 41–81). Paris: Octares et Maison des Sciences de l'Homme.

Bardram, J. (1998). Designing for the dynamics of work activities cooperative. In *Conference on Computer Supported Cooperative Work (ACA4)* (pp. 89–98).

Bedny, G., & Meister, D. (2014). *The Russian theory of activity: Current applications to design and learning*. New York: Psychology Press.

Bloom, B. S., Engelhart, M. D., Furst, E. J., Hill, W. H., & Krathwohl, D. R. (1956). Taxonomy of educational objectives: The classification of educational goals. In *Handbook I: Cognitive domain*. New York: Longmans, Green.

Bødker, S. (1989). Human activity approach to user interfaces. *Human Computer Interaction, 4*, 171–195.

Bødker, S. (1991). Through the interface-A human activity approach to user interface design. *DAIMI Report Series, 16*(224), 1–167.

Bødker, S. (1996). Applying activity theory to video analysis: How to make sense of video data in HCI. In *Context and consciousness: Activity theory and human computer interaction* (pp. 147–174). Cambridge: Massachusetts Institute of Technology Press.

Clot, Y. (1999). *La fonction psychologique du travail*. Paris: Ed. PUF.

Clot, Y. (2001). Clinique du travail et action sur soi. *Théories de l'action et éducation* (pp. 255–277). Louvain-la-Neuve: De Boeck Supérieur.

Cole, M. (1998). *Cultural psychology: A once and future discipline*. Cambridge: Harvard University Press.

Coulet, J. C. (2013). Capacités dynamiques et innovation: les apports d'un modèle psychologique des compétences individuelles et collectives. *Conf. Ass. Intern. de Management Strategique*, Nice (France). http://cdiaims2013.sciencesconf.orgconferencecdiaims2013pagescdiaims2013_coulet.pdf/.

Daniellou, F., & Rabardel, P. (2005). Activity-oriented approaches to ergonomics: Some traditions and communities. *Theoretical Issues in Ergonomics Science, 6*(5), 353–357.

Davidson, D. (1980). *Essays on actions and events*. Oxford: Clarendon Press.

de Fornel, M., & Quéré, L. (Eds.). (1999). *La logique des situations - Nouveaux regards sur l'écologie des activités sociales*. Paris: Ecole des Hautes Etudes en Science Sociales.

Dreyfus, S. E., & Dreyfus, H. L. (1980). *A five-stage model of the mental activities involved in directed skill acquisition*. Washington, DC: Storming Media. http://en.wikipedia.org/wiki/Dreyfus_model_of_skill_acquisition.

Engeström, Y. (1990). *Learning, working and imaging: Twelve studies in activity theory*. Helsinki: Orienta-Konsultit.

Engeström, Y., & Middleton, D. (1996). *Cognition and communication at work*. Cambridge: Cambridge University Press.

Engeström, Y., Miettinen, R., & Punamäki, R. L. (1999). *Perspectives on activity theory*. Cambridge and New York: Cambridge University Press.

Engeström, Y. (2006). Activity theory and expansive design. *Theories and practice of interaction design* (pp. 3–23).

Eraut, M. (2000). Non-formal learning and tacit knowledge in professional work. *British Journal of Educational Psychology, 70*, 113–136.

Faude-Koivisto, T. S., Wuerz, O., & Gollwitzer, P. M. (2009). Implementation intentions: The mental representations and cognitive procedures of if-then planning. In K. D. Markman, W. M. P. Klein, & J. A. Suhr (Eds.), *Handbook of imagination and mental simulation* (pp. 69–86). New York: Psychology Press.

Fauquet-Alekhine, Ph. (2016). Subjective ethnographic protocol for work activity analysis and occupational training improvement. *British Journal of Applied Science & Technology, 12*(5), 1–16, Article no.BJAST.21632.

Fauquet-Alekhine, Ph., & Labrucherie, M. (2012). Simulation training debriefing as a work activity analysis tool: The case of nuclear reactors pilots and civil aircraft pilots. *Socio-Organizational Factors for Safe Nuclear Operation, 1*, 79–83.

Fauquet-Alekhine, Ph., & Lahlou, S. (2017). The Square of PErceived ACtion model (SPEAC model) applied in digital ethnography for work activity analysis: Performance and workers' perception. *Current Journal of Applied Science & Technology, 22*(3), 1–13, 2017, Article no.CJAST.34985.

Fauquet-Alekhine, Ph., & Rouillac, L. (2016). The Square of PErceived ACtion model as a tool for identification, prevention and treatment of factors deteriorating mental health at work. *Journal of Mental Disorders and Treatment, 2*(3), 1–13, paper #1000126.

Fishbein, M., & Ajzen, I. (1975). *Belief, attitude, intention and behavior: An introduction to theory and research*. Reading, MA: Addison-Wesley.

Flor, N., & Hutchins, E. (1991). Analyzing distributed cognition in software teams: A case study of team programming during perfective software maintenance. In J. Koenemann-Belliveau (Ed.), *Proceedings of the Forth Annual Workshop on Empirical Studies of Programmers* (pp. 36–59). Norwood, NJ: Ablex Publishing.

Gobet, F., & Chassy, P. (2009). Expertise and intuition: A tale of three theories. *Minds and Machines, 19*, 151–180.

Gollwitzer, P. M. (1990). Action phases and mindsets. In E. T. Higgins & R. M. Sorrentino (Eds.), *Handbook of motivation and cognition: Foundations of social behavior* (pp. 51–92). New York: Guilford Press.

Gollwitzer, P. M. (2012). Mindset theory of action phases. In P. A. van Lange (Ed.), *Theories of social psychology* (pp. 526–545). Los Angeles (UA): Sage.

Halverson, C. (2002). Activity theory and distributed cognition: Or what does CSCW need to do with theories? *Computer Supported Cooperative Work, 11*, 243–267.

Heath, Ch., & Luff, P. (1991). Collaborative activity and technological design: Task coordination in London underground control rooms. In *Proceedings of the Second European Conference on Computer-Supported Cooperative Work* ECSCW'91 (pp. 65–80). Dordrecht: Springer Netherlands.

Heckhausen, H. (1991). *Motivation and action*. Heidelberg: Springer-Verlag.

Hutchins, E. (1995a). *Cognition in the wild*. Cambridge: Massachusetts Institute of Technology Press.

Hutchins, E. (1995b). How a cockpit remembers its speed. *Cognitive Science, 19*, 265–288.

Hutchins, E., & Klausen, T. (1996). Distributed cognition in an airline cockpit. In Y. Engeström & D. Middleton (Eds.), *Cognition and communication at work* (pp. 15–34). Cambridge: Cambridge University Press.

Kaptelinin, V. (1996). Computer mediated activity: Functional organs in social and developmental contexts. In B. Nardi (Ed.), *Context and consciousness, activity theory and human computer interaction*. Cambridge: Massachusetts Institute of Technology Press.

Kaptelinin, V., Kuutti, K., & Bannon, L. (1995). Activity theory: Basic concepts and applications. In Blumenthal (Ed.), *Human-computer interaction—Lecture notes in computer science*. Berlin and Heidelberg: Springer.

Kaptelinin, V., & Nardi, B. A. (1997, March). Activity theory: Basic concepts and applications. In *CHI'97 Extended Abstracts on Human Factors in Computing Systems* (pp. 158–159). ACM.

Kirsh, D. (2000). A few thoughts on cognitive overload. *Intellectica, 1*(30), 19–51.

Kongovi, M., Guzman, J. C., & Dasigi, V. (2002). Text categorization: An experiment using phrases. In *Proceedings of the 24th BCS-IRSG European Colloquium on IR Research: Advances in Information Retrieval* (pp. 213–228).

Krathwohl, D. R. (2002). A revision of Bloom's taxonomy: An overview. *Theory into Practice, 41*(4), 212–218.

Kuutti, K. (1991). Activity theory and its applications to information systems research and development. In H.-E. Nissen (Ed.), *information systems research* (pp. 529–549). Amsterdam: Elsevier Science Publishers.

Kuutti, K. (1996). Activity theory as a potential framework for human-computer interaction research. In B. Nardi (Ed.), *Context and consciousness: Activity theory and human computer interaction*. Cambridge: Massachusetts Institute of Technology Press.

Le Bellu, S. (2011). *Capitalisation des savoir-faire et des gestes professionnels dans le milieu industriel* (PhD thesis). University of Bordeau, reference 2011BOR21825.

Le Boterf, G. (1998). Évaluer les compétences - Quels jugements ? Quels critères ? Quelles instances ? *Education Permanente, 135*, 143–152.

Leontiev, A. N. /Леонтьев, А. Н. (1965). *Проблемы развития психики* [Problems of psychic development]. Москва: Мысль [Moscow: Mysl].

Leontiev, A. N. (1974). The problem of activity in psychology. *Soviet Psychology, 13*(2), 4–33.

Leontiev, A. N. /Леонтьев, А. Н. (1975). *Деятельность. Сознание. Личность* [Activity, consciousness, personality]. Москва: ЛичкоА. Е. [Moscow: LytskoA E].

Lomov, B. F. (1963). *Man and Technology* (Outlines in engineering psychology). Washington, DC: JPRS (US Department of Commerce).

Miller, G. A., Galanter, E., & Pribram, K. H. (1960). *Plans and structure and behavior*. New York: Holt Rineart & Winston.

Nardi, B. (1995). Studying context: A comparison of activity theory, situated action models, and distributed cognition. In B. Nardi (Ed.), *Context and consciousness: Activity theory and human-computer interaction* (pp. 35–52). Cambridge, MA: MIT.

Nardi, B. (Ed.). (1996). *Context and consciousness: Activity theory and human computer interaction*. Cambridge: Massachusetts Institute of Technology Press.

Norman, D. A. (1991). Cognitive artifacts. In J. Carroll (Ed.), *Designing interaction: Psychology at the human computer interface*. New York: Cambridge University Press.

Nosulenko, V., & Rabardel, P. (2007). *Rubinstein aujourd'hui. Nouvelles figures de l'activité humaine*. Paris: Octares et Maison des Sciences de l'Homme.

Ombredanne, A., & Faverge, J.-M. (1955). *L'analyse du travail. Facteur d'économie humaine et de productivité*. Paris: PUF.

Rabardel, P., & Pastré, P. (2005). *Modèles du sujet pour la conception. Dialectiques activités développements*. Toulouse: Octares.

Rogalski, J., & Samurçay, R. (1993). Task analysis and cognitive models as a framework to analyse environments for learning programming. In E. Lemut, B. Du Boulay, & G. Dettori (Eds.), *Cognitive models and intelligent environments for learning programming* (pp. 6–19). Berlin: Springer-Verlag.

Rogers, Y. (1993). Coordinating computer-mediated work. *Computer-Supported Cooperative Work, 1*, 295–315.

Rogers, Y., & Ellis, J. (1994). Distributed cognition: An alternative framework for analysing and explaining collaborative working. *Journal of Information Technology, 9*(2), 119–128.

Rubinstein, S. L. (1922). Le principe de l'activité du sujet dans sa dimension créative. In V. Nosulenko & P. Rabardel (Eds.), *Rubinstein aujourd'hui. Nouvelles figure de l'activité humaine* (pp. 129–140). Toulouse - Paris: Octarès.

Rubinstein, S. L. / Рубинштейн, С. Л. (1922). *Принцип творческой самодеятельности (к философским основам современной педагогики)* (Опубликована в журнале «Вопросы психологии», 1986, №4) [The principle of creative spontaneous activity (to philosophical principles of contemporary pedagogy) (published in the journal *The Questions of Psychology*, 1986, №4)].

Rubinstein, S. L. / Рубинштейн, С. Л. (1935). *Основы психологии: Пособие для высших педагогических учебных заведений* [Fundamentals of psychology: A handbook for higher pedagogical educational institutions]. Москва: Государственное Учебно-Педагогическое Издательство [Moscow: State Educational Pedagogical Publishing House].

Rubinstein, S. L. / Рубинштейн, С. Л. (1940). *Основы общей психологии* [Fundamentals of general psychology]. *Москва: Государственное учебно-педагогическое изд-во Министерства просвещения РСФСР* [Moscow: State Teaching and Pedagogical Publishing House of the RSFSR Ministry of Education].

Rubistein, S. L. / Рубинштейн, С. Л. (1946). *Основы общей психологии. 2-е изд* [Fundamentals of general psychology. 2nd ed.]. Москва: Государственное учебно-педагогическое изд-во Министерства просвещения РСФСР [Moscow: State Teaching and Pedagogical Publishing House of the RSFSR Ministry of Education].

Searle, J. (2001). *Rationality in action.* Cambridge: Massachusetts Institute of Technology Press.

Stuart, K. (2014). Activity theory as a reflective and analytic tool for action research on multi-professional collaborative practice. *Reflective Practice, 15*(3), 347–362.

Suchman, L. (1987). *Plans and situated actions.* The problem of human-machine communication: Cambridge University Press.

Suchman, L., & Trigg, R. (1991). Understanding practice: Video as a medium for reflection and design. In J. Greenbaum & M. Kyng (Eds.), *Design at work: Cooperative design of computer systems Hillsdale* (pp. 65–89). NJ: Lawrence Erlbaum.

Suchman, L., & Trigg, R. (1993). Artificial intelligence as craftwork. In S. Chaiklin & J. Lave (Eds.), *Understanding practice.* New York: Cambridge University Press.

Valdes Conca, J., & De Juana-Espinosa, S. (2012). The competency-based human resource management model. In *Human resources management: Concepts, methodologies, tools, and applications* (pp. 232–252). Management Association, Information Resources, IGI Global.

Ven, J. H., & Chuang, C. P. (2005). The comparative study of information competencies-using Bloom's taxonomy. *Journal of American Academy of Business, 7*(1), 136–143.

Von Bertalanffy, L. (1968). *General systems theory* (Rev ed.). New York: Braziller.

Von Cranach, M., & Kalbermatten, U. (1982). The Ordinary interactive action: Theory, methods and some empirical findings. In M. Von Cranach & R. Harre (Eds.), *The analysis of action*. London: Cambridge University Press.

Von Cranach, M., Mächler, E., & Steiner, V. (1985). The organisation of goal-directed Action: A research report. In G. P. Ginsburg, M. Brenner, & M. Von Cranach (Eds.), *Discovery strategies in the psychology of action* (pp. 19–61). London: Academic Press.

Wiener, N. (1948). *Cybernetics, or control and communication in the animal and the machine*. Paris: Hermann.

Zager, D. (2002). Collaboration as an activity. *Computer Supported Cooperative Work, 11,* 181–204.

CHAPTER 4

Refining Competencies Identification Through Digital Ethnography

Abstract This chapter explores the Cognitive Task Analysis paradigm so as to select a method for accessing competencies in action. This orients us towards "process tracing" method based on first-person video recordings of activities followed by replay subjective interviews, also known as Subjective Evidence-Based Ethnography (SEBE). The SEBE/SPEAC protocol is thus presented, argued and fully described for application to analyse activities.

Keywords Cognitive Task Analysis · Subjective Evidence-Based Ethnography · Video recording · Interview

4.1 Methods to Access Competencies in Action

Accessing competencies in action during work activity inevitably refers to work analysis and thus to the Cognitive Task Analysis paradigm which regroups methodologies for job or task design and analysis. Two reviews attempted to provide an exhaustive state of the art (Tofel-Grehl & Feldon, 2013; Wei & Salvendy, 2004) and a categorization of the methods. Moreover, Wei and Salvendy (2004) suggested guidelines in selecting Cognitive Task Analysis methods according to the aim of the studies.

P. Fauquet-Alekhine, *Knowledge Management in High Risk Industries*, https://doi.org/10.1007/978-3-030-49213-7_4

The categorization used in both reviews proposes four main categories:

- Observations and interviews:
  Providing high adaptability, these methods differ from one analysis to another because they are very sensitive to the protocol adopted (highly structured or not for instance). They are applied in real operating situations (ROS) and are task-focused.
- Process tracing:
  Capturing expertise during activity performance through audio and/or video recording, some methods may include simultaneous verbalization. They are applied in ROS and are task-focused.
- Conceptual techniques:
  These methods "refer to the products of the representations of domain concepts and their structure or interrelations to analysis tasks" (Wei & Salvendy, 2004: 276) providing composite structural representations such as conceptual graph analysis (Gordon, Schmierer, & Gill, 1993). They are indirect methods as not applied in ROS and may focus on conceptual knowledge at the expense of heuristics and strategies.
- Formal models:
  Computational models are developed to describe activities in context and are adjusted after comparison of the results with workers' feedback (e.g. Wei & Salvendy, 2000).

The guidelines in selecting Cognitive Task Analysis methods suggested by Wei and Salvendy (2004) are made up of 11 criteria. Some of the criteria regroup several conditions; this is why Table 4.1 provides 13 points (lines of the table). The aforementioned Wei and Salvendy's categories are given per column and the fulfilment of a criterion suggests adopting one or several categories for activity analysis according to the authors: they are marked by a cross in the table.

The boxes highlighted in yellow identify which methods are adapted to the types of activities to be studied: the context of the activities in complex socio-technical systems is usually well defined (for nuclear industry, see, for example, Fauquet, 2006; Fauquet-Alekhine, 2012; Fauquet-Alekhine & Maridonneau, 2016), sensitive to distraction (Fauquet-Alekhine & Boucherand, 2011, 2012, 2015) and based on knowledge, rules and skills applying well-defined procedures (Fauquet,

Table 4.1 Guidelines in selecting Cognitive Task Analysis methods suggested by Wei and Salvendy (2004)

criteria\categories	Observations and interviews	Process tracing	Conceptual techniques	Formal models
the activity domain is well defined		x		
the activity domain is NOT well defined	x			
the activity procedure is NOT well defined	x			
particular process of a task and its concurrent task performance need to be tracked		x		
data is easily captured by verbal means and data collection does not affect activity performance		x		
domain knowledge, structures, interrelations of tasks need to be defined			x	
multiple activity analysers involved, and activity analysis requires less verbalization			x	
activity needs quantitative predication, and models remain stable with context changes				x
activity performance is sensitive to distraction or interference		x	x	x
analysers do not have significant knowledge on analytical techniques	x	x	x	
activity is skill-based	x	x		
activity is rule-based		x	x	
activity is knowledge-based			x	x

Crosses in boxes indicate which categories are suitable for activity analysis when concerned by a criterion

2006; Fauquet-Alekhine, 2012, 2013, 2017a, 2017b; Fauquet-Alekhine & Maridonneau, 2016).

Wei and Salvendy's guidelines clearly lead to the conclusion:

> the most suitable, for the purpose of describing competencies in action, should be a method based on process tracing.

Among process tracing methods available to date to analyse work activities in the field, one has shown its performance (Le Bellu, Lahlou, & Nosulenko, 2010; see also Lahlou et al., 2015; Le Bellu, 2011, 2016) based on the early work of Lahlou (1999) and subsequent developments. The method implies miniature camera mounted on helmet for subjective video recordings combined to situated verbalization; recordings are analysed through a protocol based on Subjective Evidence-Based Ethnography (Lahlou, 2011). As noticed by others, video analysis may help researchers or analysts "to reveal how activities are produced with respect to the contingencies and circumstances of the participants within organizational settings, and examine how the technologies available in these domains are utilized" (Luff et al., 2013: 6.3). A similar digital ethnography technique was applied by Rieken, Garcia-Sanchez, Trujillo, and Bear (2015), using a SenseCam, with the objective of analysing a student's day at work in two police schools; the SenseCam was worn around the neck and recorded 1 image every 30 seconds throughout the working day and over 3 days.

Subjective Evidence-Based Ethnography (SEBE) was defined by Lahlou (2011). The SEBE is a family of methods developed in digital ethnography for investigation in social science based on subjective audio-video recordings (the first-person perspective: Goldman, Pea, Barron, & Derry, 2007; Knoblauch, Schnettler, Raab, & Soeffner, 2006; Lahlou, 2011; Omodei, McLennan, and Wearing, 2005; Pea, 1994; Petitmengin, 2009; Rix-Lièvre & Lièvre, 2010) using miniature video-cameras (usually worn at eye-level by subjects: the subcam). Recordings are then used for self-confrontation with subjects to collect their subjective experience, discussion of findings and final interpretations between analysts and subjects.

4.1.1 Data Collection Through Video Recordings

Using video recordings allows the work analysts access to the reality of work activities which is one of their major concerns. The use of video has almost become a necessity because the principle of cognitive economy puts subjects in a limited attention and consciousness span that makes it difficult afterwards to recall events from memory only (Lahlou, 2011: 620). According to Rieken et al. (2015: 256), "What can be more easily evaded in discussions becomes difficult to escape when data is brought to the exchange". With the video, "It is possible to identify that what the participant reports they did may be different from what they really did. This is because participants themselves contrast what they remember of a situation with what they recorded during that situation" (p. 260) and it allows one "to address practices that were actually captured, not only what they selectively recall" (p. 269). The use of video has also become a necessity because it pushes the limits of the classical observation paper/pencil: even with the help of analysis grids, the analyst's writing speed is often much slower than the performance of the task by observed workers. In addition, taking notes entails the risk of not watching the scene for a while and so missing important elements of the activity. This could be corrected by replaying the activity but in the world of work, it is generally inappropriate to ask someone to redo/repeat the activity observed several times while videoing allows for multiple visualizations retrospectively, very useful in the case of complex situations. Furthermore, playing back the video in slow motion allows a detailed analysis of the observed situation: it is sometimes useful to watch the same scene several times to understand what is happening, or at least make assumptions about what is happening. The video recording is a main tool for self-confrontation: observed subjects seeing themselves in action can learn about themselves and thus correct or improve themselves. These practices of self-analysis and reflection on action promote the development of the meta-functional activities that Falzon defines as the "activities not directly oriented towards the immediate production, activities of construction of knowledge or tools (hardware tools or cognitive tools), for possible later use, aiming at facilitating the execution of the task or at improving the performance" (Falzon, 1994 quoted by Le Bellu, 2011: 107). Thus, the video is both a source and a support: a data source for the analyst and a support of expression (body, speech), of mediation, which participates in the emergence of meaning of the activities and of the co-production of knowledge through the triangle operator-image-researcher or analyst (Falzon, 1997).

Three points of view must be considered for video recording: the third-, second- and first-person perspectives.

For the third-person perspective, the analyst uses a classical camcorder, choosing the angle of view and where to position the camera, if the camera is fixed or mobile, the number of cameras in use, when to start, when to stop. All of these choices are a series of filters that determine the result. The external camera in fact records only a selection of the real, pre-emergence of partial, biased and subjective manner, in angles chosen by the observer (Durand, 2001).

The second-person perspective is to capture a point of view that is the closest to that of the subject who performs the action, while being piloted by an outside observer with an external camera. In practice, this means that the observer moves the hand-held camera in the steps of the subject, carrying out zooms so as to be closer to the handling area which lies between the subject and the artefacts (objects, instruments, tools, colleagues, machine, documents, etc.) with which interaction is required. According to Le Bellu (2011), this technique is of relatively little interest as it is extremely intrusive to the subject observed.

The first-person perspective is to use an embedded recording device on the subject in action. The point of view of the camera is then that of the subject: this characterizes the first-person or subjective point of

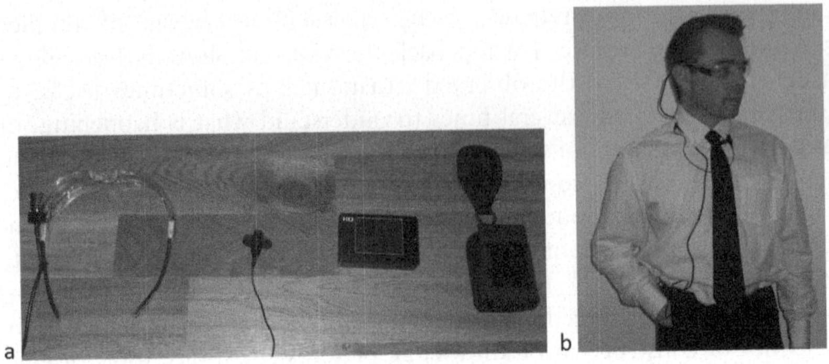

Fig. 4.1 Example of subjective camera device. **a** From left to right, mini camera on glasses, lavaliere microphone, mini-camcorder, belt holster for camcorder. **b** Equipping a subject

view. For this aim, analysts use a subcam (or subjective camera), a located shooting device that may be a camera mounted on glasses, in such a way that it is positioned as close to the subject's line of view as possible (Fig. 4.1).

The subcam automatically follows the movements of the subject's head. Thus, unlike the external camera, the subcam captures the subject's activity according to a first-person point of view through the field of view[1] and directly serves the subjectivity of the subject whose activity is studied. According to Le Bellu's work based on the pioneer studies of Lahlou (2006), the subcam is an efficient tool to access to the subject's psychology: what/why/how the subject did what he did, for what reasons, and for which goals. Looking for the capture of the gesture as closely as possible from the subject's point of view, the subcam seeks to capture the subject's vision and hearing. Activities being mostly manual, the target of information sought was within the subject's hands/arms and the technical system manipulated, interactions most often mediated by the use of tools. For most activities, it is not necessary to add

[1]The visual field is the spatial array of visual sensations available to observation in psychological experiments from the standpoint of introspections (Smythies, 1996). Visual field must not be confused with the field of view, which is everything that causes light to fall onto the retina at a given time (input), processed by the visual system and computes the visual field as the output.

an eye-tracking device to detail points of fixation of the eyes: first-person perspective gives a subfilm of the attentional stream of the subject who performs the activity and in the rare moments where this attachment point is ambiguous, the self-confrontation interview with the subject deals with this ambiguity. This allows the analyst to record even what was only visible from the subject standpoint, parts of activity that would not have been recorded by an external camera. In addition, the capture of professional sounds surrounding the subject is important because they are meaningful both in response to actions on the equipment and for decisions involving the pursuit of the gesture.

The use of a subjective perspective brought interesting series of improvements on the quality of the explanation by the operator's intentions when rendering in a self-confrontation interview with the subjective videos (Fauquet-Alekhine & Martinez, 2020; Lahlou, 2006). Le Bellu (2011) and Lahlou et al. (2015) have suggested that this was due to the activation of episodic memory: in the line of Tulving's standpoint (1972, 2002), Le Bellu wrote that it is only memory system that allows people to consciously re-experience past experiences. The trace of the activity offered by the first-person perspective can be seen as an ally of memory, when coming back to the recorded activity. Subjects are thus put back into the action which helps them to remember, to rebuild the reasoning applied during the realization of the visualized actions.

Lahlou et al. (2015: 5) explained: "It seems that the more similar the context of memory retrieval is to the context of memory encoding, the better is the recall, and that having multimodal cues helps, especially when they are spatial or motor - see the enactment effect (Engelkamp & Cohen, 1991). In other words, re-living the situation from a first-person perspective would facilitate recalling one's own actions and mental states/processes. This considerably simplifies analysis and interpretation, as well as validating/falsifying research hypotheses".

4.1.2 *Data Analysis Through Confrontation with Subjective Video*

Analysing data within the SEBE framework implies confronting the subject to the subjective video through a subjective replay interview (RIW). This stage of the analysis is essential since according to Leplat (2000), observing an activity says little about the intentions, considered options and the mental operations of the subject. Hence, video data is not sufficient to achieve the objective of capitalization and transfer of knowledge.

In particular, they give no information about the subject's perception neither of the situation nor of the element of the work context that guide decision-making processes. Moreover, they give no direct access to non-observable knowledge or know-how, which seems inaccessible because of tacit knowledge.

Confronting the subject with the subjective video as done in the SEBE framework refers to situational approaches in that they favour the setting in the foreground of the subject in a situation. They are opposed to non-situational approaches (Coolican, 2009; Crane & Hannibal, 2009; Denning, 2004; Garcia-Lorenzo, 2010; Oddone, Re, & Briante, 1981) which adopt a more distant view of the situation by providing methodological tools more centred on reports or preparations of activities and/or past and future events.

Subjective replay interview or RIW (Lahlou, 2011) takes from techniques of self-confrontation[2] developed by Von Cranach, Kalbermatten, Indermühle, and Gugler (1982) and later by Theureau (2002) as a method of investigation of human activity in the framework of his theory of goal-oriented activity and explicitation interview (Vermersch 1994) which is a descriptive verbal implementation of action experienced by a subject. The RIW method is similar to the cued recall debrief developed by Omodei and McLennan (1994) and applied by others (see, for example, Bentley, Johnston, & Baggo, 2005; Rix & Biache 2004). It aims at explaining the subjects' activity based on the video recording of their activity according to a subjective situational point of view. Subjective video is used as a medium of consecutive interview: particular sequences of the video are chosen by the analyst and subjects are asked to comment on them. During the subjective re-situ interview, the objective trace provided by the video recording constitutes a stable and reliable basis for the production by the subject of a comment relating to his/her activity and more precisely relating to the act viewed in situation (Theureau, 2002; Rix & Biache, 2004). The associated cognitive process is well described by Lahlou: "The subcam provides material that is especially relevant for the reconstruction of the mental activity. Experience shows that subjects are often able, even weeks after the fact, to recall the situation very precisely. We can check whether this is not a reconstruction by asking

[2]When confronting several participants' standpoints (case a collaborative activity for instance), the method applied is cross-confrontation (Clot, 1999; Clot, Faïta, Fernandez, & Scheller, 2001; Mollo & Falzon, 2004).

the subject 'what will happen next', and then compare with the actual action on film. This recall effect is probably due to the nature of episodic memory (Tulving, 1972, 2002). While semantic memory recalls general relations between objects, episodic memory is a multimodal association connected to an actual lived event (time, place, associated emotions, intentions, contextual knowledge and other associations), which come back as a bundle when the subject recalls the event. Viewing his own film, when put back into an exact relationship with the actual lived sequence, the subject is naturally induced to recall this sequence. Getting multimodal cues allows much better recovery of the events experienced [...]. At this stage, it is possible to have access to the thoughts and emotions of the subject (Bentley, Johnston, & Baggo, 2005) even weeks later, a delay often needed for the analysis and arranging an appointment with the subject. Such an effect is observed with classical film recording, but not to the same degree as with the subcam" (Lahlou, 2011: 623). What is specific in the replay interview as practised by Lahlou and the SEBE-Lab team (www.SEBE-Lab.net) is the use of Activity Theory and situated and Distributed Cognition in the formulation of the questions asked to the participant, which make the participant explain the goals, motives and influence of the affordances provided in situation in the construction of action.

4.2 SEBE/SPEAC Protocol

The overall structure of the protocol complies to a classic frame of process tracing: capturing activity through video recording and analysing activity through reflexive analysis.

4.2.1 Comments About Capturing the Activity

We need to have access to a description of the gestures and of the activity, and referring to the Activity Theory, the analysis is related to the level of the action unit in context. Yet the spontaneity of the activity has to be preserved as much as possible to ensure access to tacit knowledge in situation: for Polanyi (1967), tacit knowledge is intuitive and spontaneous (Wasonga & Murphy, 2006), and at the collective level, it comes from the improvisation that summons the group of individuals in context (Erden, von Krogh, & Nonaka, 2008). We need to adopt an approach in the frame of "naturalistic studies of work, interaction and technology", which helps analysts to take into account both tools and artefacts seriously, as well as the complex array of information they provide in action and social interaction (Heath & Hindmarsh, 2002). Therefore, a significant preparation work before video recording the activity is proscribed as well as simultaneous verbalization which slows down the activity as shown by Le Bellu (2011).

Subcam—First-person perspective
Regarding the miniature camera, a model like GoPro mounted on helmet must be rejected because not adapted for field workers: during their job in an industrial field, they move a lot, sometimes between or under ducts, bend over equipment or descend/climb caged ladders; in this context, the camera-helmet is cumbersome, can cling and unbalance, and after a while may be heavy. However, as safety glasses are mandatory in the field, a cylindrical miniaturized camera mounted on safety glasses is suitable. The safety glasses used by workers in the fields have to meet industrial safety standards so that they can be protected against mechanical choc or liquid or particle projection (including chemical products). A wireless device must be rejected to avoid any electromagnetic interference with the control-command of the industrial process.

We selected devices provided by Active Media Concept (www.amc-tec.com) (Fig. 4.1):

- A square miniaturized camera 170-5MP (12 × 12 mm, 20 mm length), 600 lines colour, 170° angle lens, which we mounted on safety glasses.
- Additional lavaliere microphone although the miniaturized camera had its own integrated microphone (this precaution was to ensure a good audio quality.
- Micro audio digital recorder DVR-500-HD2 providing HD video recording up to 1280 × 960 pixels at 25 frames per second, integrated touch 3" colour display (this permits a real-time view of what is filmed and an easy control of the camcorder), three timestamp recording modes (motion detection, continuous, programmed), remote control wired and infrared (not used if there is any risk of electromagnetic interferences), SDHC memory expandable up to 32 GB, USB connection.

These specifications are a minimum to obtain a satisfactory definition of the videos and a satisfactory view of what subjects do, including viewing the document they read. Other solutions may be found at the SEBE-Lab (contact at www.SEBE-Lab.net).

When this SEBE equipment is used, subjects often asked questions regarding this equipment performance and, in some cases, tell us about their own equipment for subjective video like GoPro camera or Google glasses. The subsequent question is often why we do not use this kind of material (about 100 euros) while it is less expensive than the equipment selected (about 700 euros) presented on Fig. 4.1 and more compact. Regarding GoPro, the problem is mainly the bulk: the camera cannot be worn in the field as explained above. Regarding Google glasses (as well as any similar equipment) with all the hardware integrated into the frame and stems of the glasses including the camera in the middle of the front structure, the design implies to use exclusively these glasses. In case of subjects wearing vision glasses or in case of need to wear specific glasses as Personal Protective Equipment due to risks induced by the work activity, Google glasses cannot be worn and thus the capture cannot be undertaken. This remark leads to another issue: What is the best solution to mount the miniaturized camera on the glasses? We prospected to find a fast removable system adaptable to any glasses in vain. Finally, the best solution is the simplest and less expensive: the electrical adhesive tape to stick the subcam on the stem of the safety glasses.

Subcam for a second-person perspective

For workers moving here and there in the field, the observer has to follow the subject in the field in order to have an external point of view of the activity. A camcorder in hand may be a solution, but this would leave only one hand free for the observer who generally takes notes.

The solution may be to use a subcam worn by the observer. Doing so, the observer obtains second-person perspective movies of the field workers with hands free.

Camcorder—Third-person perspective

The third-person perspective is sometimes mandatory. It may be expected to complete the first-person perspective with contextual data as done by Le Bellu (2011) for example; the necessity of multiple videos records was pointed out by Luff and Heath (2012).

For third-person perspective capture, the point of view of the camera must be carefully chosen: too close to the subjects would not give enough information because some actions or interactions would not be watched, and too far would not allow the observers to watch some of them. The adapted point of view is called "mid-shot" (Luff & Heath, 2012: 262), a medium distance that "typically captures the activities of two or three people". However, when subjects move in the field (case of field workers in industries or police officers in the town), third-person perspective may be difficult to carry out.

Bias due to second- or third-person perspective
Capturing subjects' activity through video recording, whatever the perspective chosen is, generates a bias to the naturalistic character of the situations. Naturalistic observation assumes studied subjects are in their state and/or natural environment; the observer avoiding the subjects notices that they are observed because this may change their behaviour. Insofar as the subjects know they are observed when they carry an audio and video recording device or when they see in certain circumstances the observer at short distance: the observation is intrusive.

To reduce this bias, it is strongly recommended to leave out the second- and third-person perspectives and only use the first-person perspective video.

4.2.2 Comments About the Interview

Based on the SPEAC model, the structure of the replay interview is designed as follows:

- Before watching the subjective video, the two poles *Having to act* and *Knowing to act* are questioned.
- A subjective replay interview is performed watching the subjective video.
- After watching the subjective video, the two poles *Wanting to act* and *Being able to act* are questioned.

As pointed out above, the two poles *Having to act* and *Knowing to act* are mainly defined by the organization before doing the activity: the worker is usually aware of what he/she has to do before performing the activity due to the prescription, the procedure related to the task and the manager's order, and he/she knows to do it because, as a professional identified to perform this task, he/she "obviously" had an occupational training for this purpose. The prescription, the manager's order, as well as the professional training are for a great part defined before performing the activity through the task definition and the worker's official qualification. Therefore, during the interview, it is interesting to question these two poles before watching the subjective video so that viewing the video does not influence the content of the answers: the subject is positioned as in the operating situation, as if the context of the activity was about to be discovered. On the contrary, the poles *Wanting to act* and *Being able to act* may be thought by the worker before performing the activity, but they may be continuously and significantly adjusted to the situation while performing the activity. These poles are less pre-defined by the organization than the two others. For the subjective video to remind the worker how performing the activity influenced the poles *Wanting to act* and *Being able to act*, they are questioned after the viewing in the frame of the interview.

The structure of the SEBE/SPEAC-based replay interview offers subsequently an interesting possibility: on the one hand by analysing the difference between answers to questions from one another, and on the other hand by analysing the difference between answers to questions and the resulting content of the replay interview, the analyst could identify tacit knowledge and differentiate it from explicit knowledge. Illustrating this possibility by referring to the previous example, when a subject describes the action "going to the fast food" through *Knowing to act*, crossing the street will probably not be mentioned. But when viewing the details of the subjective video of the action, comments such as "I'm crossing the street looking left and right" might be made if the scene were to take place in New York City. Crossing the street watching left and right refers to competencies related to tacit knowledge. If one of the subject's friends comes for the first time to visit the subject from Paris and ask to go alone to the fast food, the subject will likely not explain how to cross the street.

4.2.3 *Structure of the Protocol*

The SEBE/SPEAC protocol is applied to occupational activities with minimum preparation of the subjects in order not to decrease the spontaneity of the realization and favour access to tacit knowledge in situations. For the same reason, no anticipated or simultaneous verbalization is required. The protocol is structured in three phases: preparation phase, capture phase and analysis phase.

Preparation phase
The preparation phase is a distant contact with the potential participants. It is structured in two steps:

- Identification of the activity occurrence and of the situation.
  - Overall risk analysis undertaken by the analysts and managers to identify the activities concerned and the factors that might hinder one of the parties not to reach its goals. This must often be made several weeks in advance.
  - The analyst may meet the potential participants in order to give them an insight of what will be done.
- Negotiation with the management to carry out the investigation.
  - When the activity and the participants are identified, the management is contacted to negotiate time for capture and time for interviews. This must be agreed early to be sure having time for replay interviews: during capture, workers work as usual, not during interviews.

Capture phase
The capture phase is a direct contact with the participants. It is structured in four steps:

- Informing participants and obtaining informed consent about the capture phase.
  - This step is brief for the following activity to be as spontaneous as possible (less than 10 min).
  - Information includes what their contributions are for, how the analyst may disturb them during the observation, what is done with videos (analysis), how it is used (ethics).
- Installation of external and subjective video devices; framing (less than 10 min).
- Capture (subcam and camcorder) of the raw activity not commented (from 15 min to several hours).
- Storage of material and immediate short feedback; making appointments for the replay interview (less than 10 min):

- The main goal of the immediate short feedback is to thank participants, remind them what their contributions are for, how it is used (ethics), what is expected from analysis.
- The appointments are scheduled within one week at the most and as close to the capture phase as possible.

Analysis phase

The analysis phase is structured in four steps:

- Pre-viewing of the recordings without participants and selection by the analyst of particular sequences of the video for subjects to comment on them.
- Replay interview with participants (about one hour per interview):
  - Informing participants and obtaining informed consent about the analysis phase.
  - Replay interview (recorded) with first actor of the situation.
  - Replay interview (recorded) with second actor of the situation in case of analysing a collaborative activity with two workers.
  - Replay interview (recorded) with both actors of the situation in case of analysing a collaborative activity with two workers.
  - The replay interview (RIW) is a SEBE/SPEAC-based structure adopting a sequenced questioning:

    First RIW sequence: Before watching the subjective video, the two poles *Having to act* and *Knowing to act* are questioned.

    Second RIW sequence: The interview is performed watching the subjective video. The subjects are instructed to describe their activity but also to announce their goals, or intentions, objectives. These different terms are used as synonyms in order to remove any ambiguity in the term “goal”. The subjects are free during the viewing to stop it when they want to facilitate the comment of a selected passage.

    Third RIW sequence: After watching the subjective video, the two poles *Wanting to act* and *Being able to act* are questioned.
  - Replay interviews are consecutive goal-oriented verbalizations which look for:

    The subjects’ feelings including the disturbance eventually induced by the protocol or the devices.

    The subjects’ goals and sub-goals before and during the activity realization.

The subjects' conscious mental representations of the expected results: individual and (not) shared representations.
The individual representation of collaborative activity.
How the activity is structured, at an individual level and collective level.
How the activity is performed at an individual level and collective level.
The (not) existing factors of coordination.
Subjects' interactions.
The subjects' conscious mental representations of tools.
Subjects' perspective-taking in case of collaborative activity.
Perspective-taking models (Gillespie & Richardson, 2011; Krauss & Fussell, 1989; Krauss & Weinheimer, 1967) allow the understanding of the context of communication between interactants from the representation that they were organizing in alternated point of views subject/interactant. The shared understanding of the context is so built by varying the point of reference, each interactant taking the place of the other. Gillespie and Richardson (2011) gave evidences of performance gain for cooperative activity when perspective-taking was applied as opposed to cases it was not.

- Post-analysis of the replay interviews by the analyst aiming at understanding:
  - The individual (and, if several co-workers, collective) representation of (respectively collaborative) activity through the main (respectively mutual) goal.
  - Subjects' perspective-taking and consequences.
  - The mapping out of the shared knowledge and associated communication vectors at both individual and collective levels.
  - Sets of competencies required for each worker and related explicit and tacit knowledge and know-how.
    Individual and collective aspects are considered.
    This results in the matrix of competencies for the studied activity.
    The construction of the matrix of competencies follows strict but simple rules. The analysis of the replay interviews makes it possible to identify the various fields of competencies necessary to put competencies successfully in action. These fields of competencies are identified on the basis of goals and sub-goals described by subjects during the RIW. For each of these fields distributed by column in the matrix, knowledge and know-how are identified

Table 4.2 Example of draft for a matrix of competencies per profession

Fields of competencies	Field "Call for help"	...
K (in order to KH) individual explicit or tacit	Knowing your own limits to know how to recognize that the problem is outside your own competencies.(*) Knowing the limits of your job to recognize that the problem is out of job competencies.(*)	...
K (in order to KH) collective explicit or tacit	Knowing the domains of work per professions to know how to identify the professions which can give help.(*)	...

(*) Each sentence implies knowing (K) something in order to know-how (KH) to do something

and input in this column (Table 4.2). Each knowledge is associated with know-how expressed in the form of a sentence containing two propositions separated by the expression "in order to" such as "knowing something in order to know how to do something else" where "in order" may be omitted to lighten the sentence. The first part of the sentence describes a knowledge and the second a know-how. Example: "knowing your own limits (in order) to recognize that the problem is out of own skills". The first "knowing" of the sentence can be replaced by a synonym or a synonym expression, e.g. quoting, being aware of, ...

The fields of competencies and associated knowledge and know-how are finally analysed according to the position within the replay interview of the elements and clues that permitted their identification. Due to the SEBE/SPEAC-based structure of the replay interview (sequenced questioning), this allows the analyst to categorize knowledge and know-how as tacit, explicit, individual or collective. In theory, this is obtained by comparing the answers provided by the subject before, during and after viewing the subjective video: for example, an element of knowledge not told while answering the pole *Knowing to act* but revealed later may be assumed to be tacit. However, we shall see that in practice, the method works a bit differently (see Sect. 4.2.4 "Subtleties of application of the SEBE/SPEAC protocol").

Example: Knowing the process for updating and archiving the Modus Operandi (MO) in order to guarantee the validity of the MO in hands.

This is the kind of knowledge which is not spontaneously mentioned by a worker describing the field of competencies for the activity "applying a MO".

Table 4.3 Insight of a typical matrix resulting from the SEBE/SPEAC analysis for the activity "applying a Modus Operandi (MO)"

Fields of competencies	Field #1: [Knowing how to] use a MO	Field #2: ...	...
Individual Knowledge and Know-How	1-Knowing the rules required to frame and to write a MO [in order to know how] to read it and understand it 2- Knowing the process so as to update and archive a MO [in order to know how] to guarantee the validity of the MO used 3-... ...	1-... 2-... ...	...
Collective Knowledge and Know-How	1-... 2-... ...	1-... 2-... ...	...

NB: Tacit knowledge and know-how are highlighted in yellow

- Validation (about one hour).
  - The findings of the post-analysis are shared with the actors.
  - It helped the analyst to validate the conclusions.
  - It helped the participants to have a feedback about their knowledge and know-how as tacit, explicit, individual or collective and eventually to improve their meta-knowledge about the activity.

An additional step can be added in order to share the findings and conclusions with the team usually interested in the analysis and the results.

The resulting product of the SEBE/SPEAC analysis is a matrix listing per columns the fields of competencies identified (Table 4.3). For each column, knowledge and know-how are listed, first regarding the individual aspect and then regarding the collective aspect. During the post-analysis, these assumed to be tacit are highlighted in yellow. After the validation phase, the expression of the knowledge and know-how may be modified, some may be withdrawn and others added; for example, the analyst may have identified a knowledge as tacit whereas the worker identifies it as part of the fundamentals of the professions systematically taught within the initial training programme for the novices; in this case, the item is withdrawn from the matrix but integrated into another matrix addressing the basic knowledge and know-how regarding the profession. For example, "knowing how to read a procedure" can be considered as part of the core knowledge of a profession, to be known by a technician whatever the activity is, and thus withdrawn from the matrix of competencies specific to the activity "setting up the neutral point of the pneumatic valve".

The rules for the construction of the matrix are grounded by the KKHS model (Chapter 2):

- Field of competencies
  It designates a general know-how and thus is expressed beginning with "knowing how to" followed by the infinitive of an action verb. So as to simplify the table, "knowing how to" may be omitted. This is why it is written between brackets in the example in Table 4.3. Therefore, the expression of a field of competencies begins with the infinitive of an action verb.
- Knowledge and Know-how
  It refers to what subjects keep in memory after having had an access to some information (lessons, books, demonstration...). It is expressed by the gerundive form of the verb "to know" followed by direct object. According to the KKHS model, knowledge fosters know-how. It is thus expected to be followed by the expression "in order to know how to" and the infinitive form of an action verb. However, in the aim to lighten the matrix, "in order to know how to" may be omitted. This is why it is written between brackets in the example in Table 4.3.
  Similarly, according to the KKHS model, know-how is fostered by knowledge. It is thus expected to be preceded by the expression of knowledge.
  In addition, knowledge may be expressed by the verb "to know" as well as by any other synonym or expression. For example, the following may be admitted: know, be conscious of, be aware of. Other verbs may depict the acquisition of knowledge in real time: read, check, repeat.

4.2.4 *Subtleties of Application of the SEBE/SPEAC Protocol*

The SEBE/SPEAC protocol draws strength mainly from the subjective video-based interview and the sequenced questioning (the three phases of the RIW).

As often discussed in the present book, using a subjective video combines the advantage of recalling the actions through the video and the advantage of a recall from a first-person perspective. This has already been argued and will not be discussed again here.

Applying the SEBE/SPEAC protocol in experimental or applicative conditions (see next chapters) shows that, in practice, the protocol works differently for some points than what had been assumed theoretically when elaborating the protocol.

In theory, the access to knowledge or know-how is supposed to be favoured by the replay subjective and goal-oriented approach of the interviews. In practice, this was verified in our studies (the results demonstrate it in Fauquet-Alekhine, 2016a; Fauquet-Alekhine & Lahlou, 2017) and was also demonstrated by Le Bellu et al. (2010). Regarding this point, theory and practice converge.

In theory, the access to tacit knowledge or know-how is supposed to emerge from the comparison between the answers given by the subjects during the first sequence of the RIW (questioning the poles *Having to act* and *Knowing to act*) and the following sequences of the RIW. The access to tacit knowledge is thus supposed to emerge from a rational comparison: it was assumed that what is said in the following sequences but not said during the first sequence might be considered as tacit. Strictly applying such a rule would lead to identifying a lot of explicit knowledge and know-how as tacit while they are explicit. This is due to the fact that, whatever the time spent carrying out the first sequence and even when using a large panel of indirect questions, subjects cannot recall all that is explicit to them or do not mention what is obvious in their opinion; for example, knowing how to handle a valve in order to close it may not be discussed whereas some valves close the other way round to others. The difficulty here is that in this first sequence of the RIW, no video support is used. Consequently, in practice, explicit as well as tacit matter emerges throughout the course of the interview, especially during the sequence when the subjective video is viewed. It is then the analyst's duty to be shrewd enough to seize clues during the exchange that suppose the identification of a tacit knowledge and know-how and to re-question at this moment the poles *Having to act* and *Knowing to act*. This shows all the importance for the analysts to constantly keep in mind the polar structure of the SPEAC model during the interview. The post-analysis of the recorded interview allows the analysts to identify and differentiate tacit from explicit. However, the work is not completed. The tacit matter is labelled as "possible": indeed, what is identified as "tacit" by the analysts during post-analysis might be elements considered by the subjects as basic knowledge (the trivial fundamentals of the profession), and for this reason, the subjects might not have spontaneously mentioned them. This is why the restitution-validation phase is so important: it is the moment for the analysts to present and discuss the output matrix to the subjects and validate the matter identified as well as their respective status: explicit or tacit. Only the professionals concerned can decide on the issue.

Complementing the SPEAC model
Another point of importance, which might be considered as a limit of the SEBE/SPEAC protocol, is that it might be restrictive if used without considering the interaction of the analysed activity with the other constituents of the socio-technical system in which it is carried out. "Restrictive" means that the analysis might be exclusively or excessively focused on the subject due to the subject-oriented nature of the protocol: questions are asked using "you" and the collected data is subjective. Despite the exogenous character of some of the poles of the SPEAC model, when answering the questions, the subject might focus on a particular aspect of the pole. For example, *Being able to act* relates to means and to the help that other professions might provide; in case of problems occurring with tools while carrying out the activity, the subject might omit to talk about the needs of other professions.

A way of addressing this limitation is to guarantee a macro-approach of the analysis by forcing the analyst to consider the subject as an interactional entity within an organizational system; the aim is to be sure to question and thus include interactions, for example, with other professions equipment and tools related to the subjects' activity. To do so, the set of indirect questions (see appendix) used to question the poles must be carefully elaborated.

Among the possible tools likely to permit a macro-approach of the activity, we selected the model of Engeström (Engeström, 2006;

Engeström & Sannino, 2010 quoting Engeström, 1987: 78) reproduced on Fig. 3.3 (Chapter 3). The choice was oriented by the synthetic conception of the model combined to its detailed representation of the possible interactions between workers, workers' actions and the socio-technical system. Considering the possible interactions suggested by the model, the set of indirect questions for the SPEAC model was consequently enriched.

In practice, not all these indirect questions can apply because of depending on the activity and the context. To save time, we suggest analysts to select the relevant questions before the RIW. This is especially useful when the management accept to free workers for no more than a one-hour RIW.

Linguistic aspects of the replay interview

The language used by subjects to describe their work activity is not innocuous and may even be a source for understanding the activity beyond the literal meaning of the words or sentences. Psycholinguistic studies have been undertaken regarding discourse analysis and communication in the workplace (see, for example, Andrén, Sanne, & Linel, 2010; Cameron & Webster, 2005; Fauquet-Alekhine, 2009, 2010, 2017a, 2017b; Limaye, 1992; Roth, 2004) and have contributed to the demonstration that language through the discourse or the narrative may carry implicit depictions of the subjects' activities. Among these implicit elements of language, metaphors may offer new angles of comprehension of the subjects' activity (Bogusławski, 1994; Glucksberg, 2003; Goddard, 2004; Lakoff, 1993; Lakoff & Johnson, 1980a, 1980b, 2003; Steen, 2011; Veraksa, 2013).

Therefore, the detection and analysis of metaphorical language as a tool for work analysis during the replay interview is an aspect which should be studied in more depth. An example presented by Fauquet-Alekhine and Daviet (2015) demonstrates its capacity to contribute towards the identification of tacit knowledge. The article reports how a nuclear reactor pilot described the way he was getting information in the control room (activity named "block-watch around"). During the replay interview, the pilot emphasized the way he was checking recorders; this was done using a metaphorical expression: the pilot said "je regarde si ça tire droit" (I watch whether it goes straight). This meant the pilot did not read the values of parameters on the recorders. He confirmed this point when asked and explained that for certain recorders or indicators, it was easy and fast to check a signal position rather than read the value according to the scale of the recorder and compare it with the expected value. This was done without losing any reliability on values. This gave rise to further analysis (Fauquet-Alekhine & Daviet, 2015; Fauquet-Alekhine, 2020).

Nevertheless, this aspect of the discourse has not yet been sufficiently explored regarding work activity analysis (see, for example, Wasonga & Murphy, 2006).

Psychological issues of the SEBE/SPEAC protocol

Beyond the psychological and cognitive processes discussed all along the previous sections and focusing on the way the SEBE/SPEAC protocol may help analysts to access what makes competencies of workers, side effects were observed and are worth being mentioned here.

A positive aspect addresses the benefits perceived by subjects for themselves just after the replay interviews. After our experiments and applications, subjects had a positive feeling following the RIW and said they were enthusiastic about this sort of analysis. Most of them explained to be very pleased to have had such an exchange during the RIW and to have viewed the video. This helped them to identify some weaknesses regarding their professional practices and to discover tacit knowledge they were not considering because it was unconscious. Beyond this qualitative feedback, a quantitative assessment has confirmed it and the results are presented in Chapter 5, Sect. 5.4 "Acceptance of the Protocol by Participants".

A potential negative aspect was also observed following one of the collective replay interviews between a reactor pilot and a field worker at a French nuclear power plant. This issue was linked with the intersubjective structure analysis during the collective replay interview. The pilot and the field worker had both independently completed an individual RIW during which precise moments of the work activity had been examined to assess the coherence of the intersubjective structure of collaboration (see the study addressing collaborative work in Fauquet-Alekhine & Lahlou, 2020). As for any replay interview, none of them knew how the colleague had assessed the perspective-taking (the way how they perceive themselves working with the co-worker and how they perceive the co-worker working with them): the collective interview which followed was precisely made to confront their respective standpoints, to obtain additional information regarding these standpoints and to enhance their perspective-taking, ex post facto. The collective interview was held during a nightshift in the operations department at 01:00 a.m., in an office located one floor above the control room. The nightshifts beginning at 09:45 p.m. and ending at 06:15 a.m., the interview took place sometime during the shift in accordance with the subjects' workload. During the collective interview, while the analyst and the two participants had viewed both excerpts of their subfilms regarding a specific moment for which they expressed different perspective-taking (e.g. one considering they were collaborating, the other that they were not collaborating), the analyst asked them what made this difference in their opinion. What is interesting here is not what they answered but how they said it. It was clear that the field worker was trying to excuse the pilot's difference in opinion while the pilot's behaviour, facial expressions and speech depicted a kind of guilt. At the same time, the pilot, trying to argue his position (including long silences), seemed to be ready to change his assessment. However, these details were not discussed during the interview, just discreetly noted by the analyst. The exchange regarding this particular point took a third of the interview time. What is interesting now is what this induced in the following minutes. At the end of this collective interview, i.e. around 01:40 a.m. in this case, the pilot and the field worker went back to their work. Usually, the pilot goes back to the control room with the field worker, and after an exchange to agree and prepare the following activities, the field worker goes back to the field. This takes 10 min. However, on this night, half an hour after the end of the collective interview, the analyst went to the control room in order to find a new participant for a next interview. Surprisingly, the field worker met in the previous interview was still there and, more surprising, the pilot and the field worker were still discussing their opposing standpoint regarding their irrespective intersubjective structure of collaboration. It was clear that the past exchange had created a kind of discomfort between the participants. It was also clear that the analyst had to take time for an additional exchange in order to make sure the colleagues would still be able to work together and this was done. The following night, the analyst tried to meet them again. Only the field worker was present as the pilot was having a day-off. The field worker accepted to come and exchange ideas about the previous night event in an individual interview which was held at 01:00 a.m. The issue of a possible tension created between the field worker and the pilot due to the RIW was addressed; the field worker declared: "in my opinion 'no problem' since we made jokes [yesterday] after [our discussion]" and he added that he thought they would laugh about it when he [the pilot] comes back to work. And what about the same situation with a pilot that the field worker would not like? The field worker explained at once that he would not have gone in the control room the previous night to discuss such a topic with someone he does not like and added: "we are not forced to like people with whom we work anyway". This short individual interview ended on the conclusion that there was no problem between the field worker and the pilot.

This storytelling points out the possible tension that the collective RIW might generate between co-workers in case of diverging points of view regarding their professional activity. This may create the starting point of a tension that might never be defused if the co-workers never discuss it. Perhaps no real conflict will emerge directly from this situation, but it may be one additional factor contributing to feed a future conflict.

The conclusion of the episode is that the analysts must be aware of such potential problem so as to be sensitive to details that would elude them and to manage the situation as necessary if applicable.

4.3 Performance of the SEBE/SPEAC Protocol

The SPEAC model, the resulting protocol, the results and conclusions of the tests and applications were published in journals (Fauquet-Alekhine, 2016a, 2016b; Fauquet-Alekhine & Lahlou, 2017, 2020; Fauquet-Alekhine et al., 2018).

4.3.1 *How Many Situation Cases to Observe to Access What Makes Competencies of Workers?*

To date, all workers participating in the experiments and applications were experienced workers except one. Three findings are worth mentioning and contribute to answer the question:

- Observing an experienced worker and analysing the activity in detail using the SEBE/SPEAC protocol does not require many cases.

We compared analyses of similar activities performed in the nuclear industry. Each similar activity gave the same results in terms of the knowledge and know-how identified. Therefore, one activity was sufficient to describe an activity with systematized methods, standardized procedures and stable means.

- Observing a novice worker supervised by an experienced worker may or may not bring additional relevant details when compared with the case of an experienced worker: when applying the SEBE/SPEAC protocol to such a case, the additional details obtained mainly concerned the experienced worker supervising a novice rather than the novice's work.
- Observing the workers in simulated situations (SimS) does not provide all data of the real operating situations (ROS). For a given work activity, the comparison between SimS and ROS showed a difference in terms of the amount of knowledge and know-how identified as well as in terms of the nature of these. The ROS provided more data regarding the collective dimension of the activity and the SimS provided data devoted to the simulator even though it may be expressed in the same way as for the ROS. For example, knowing how to use the procedure may be different in SimS and ROS if procedures are not presented with the same standard; knowing how to assess the correctness of a quantity may be different if the calculator for the monitoring of some parameters on a simulator is unable to reflect the real physical process with accuracy. The conclusion is that the SEBE/SPEAC protocol needs ROS to improve ROS. Perhaps we should say it differently: the SEBE/SPEAC protocol needs the situations for which competencies are sought.

The protocol was also applied at school (see Chapter 5): the performance of a cohort of students in Economical and Social Science was significantly improved after analysing the activity of one clever student in ROS. This came to confirm the results obtained in the world of work.

4.3.2 *Comparing the SEBE/SPEAC Protocol with Other Methods*

The SEBE/SPEAC protocol was applied to analyse work activities at a French nuclear power plant during ROS of Operation shift teams (15 situations and 30 participants, about 1950 min video recordings and 2400 min audio recordings) and during SimS. Results were compared with those obtained with the self-confrontation and with the standard method applied in the French nuclear fleet (Systematic Approach to Training (SAT) developed in 1996 by the International Atomic Energy Agency (IAEA, 1998)). All the methods provided knowledge and know-how necessary to perform work activities. The SEBE/SPEAC protocol showed a significantly higher level of identification of knowledge and know-how per activity (from 1.9 to 9 times more) than self-confrontation or SAT and at a lower cost (mainly less people involved). In particular, collective or tacit knowledge and know-how were easier to identify with the SEBE/SPEAC protocol. Results are published and discussed in Fauquet-Alekhine (2016a) and Fauquet-Alekhine and Lahlou (2017, 2020).

4.3.3 Using Other Methods Than the SEBE/SPEAC Protocol to Access Knowledge and Know-How

This point addresses the usefulness of the SEBE/SPEAC protocol to access knowledge and know-how through process tracing. In other words, could another method lead to the same results? We are tempted to answer "yes" provided that:

- A first-person perspective video is used for analysis.
- The activity is captured in naturalistic situations.
- The interview is of the self-confrontation type.
- The SPEAC model is underpinning the structure of the interview or at least the analyst's questions for the interview; this means that the analyst must permanently bear in mind the four poles of the SPEAC model.

However, in such conditions, it becomes difficult to find a method differing from the SEBE/SPEAC protocol.

Regarding the first point, the benefits of the first-person perspective video were identified, commented, argued and explained in the previous chapters and that will not be done here again.

Regarding the second point, this favours access to tacit knowledge and know-how.

Regarding the third point, the self-confrontation is a mandatory way to lead an interview based on a first-person perspective video. This is to create a reflexive analysis of the activity.

Regarding the fourth point, the main thing is to keep in mind the existence of the four interactional poles of the SPEAC model making successful competencies in action. Indeed, this helps the analyst to ask the relevant and appropriate questions during the interview. This means that integrating the SPEAC model inside other protocols of the SEBE category or even, more widely, inside other methods of the "Process tracing" category identified in Cognitive Task Analysis (Table 4.1) should contribute to improve the results; the assumption of improvement is based on the capacity to access data through a SPEAC model-based interview.

4.4 Limitations of the SEBE/SPEAC Protocol

Biases and limits of the SEBE/SPEAC Protocol
Rieken et al. (2015: 256) pointed out that "Just as the presence of a researcher can affect respondents' actions (Wickström and Bendix 2000), so might the presence of the recording device change the behaviour of recording and recorded individuals". This was actually pointed out during our applications at two levels:

- The third-person video recording: this approach was abandoned because of the need to preserve the subjects' spontaneity to access tacit competencies. At first, it was assumed that this would yield loss of relevant information to understand the activity, but the course of the applications showed that the first-perspective video combined with the subjects' comments was sufficient to reach a satisfactory level of information. The results obtained in terms of performance may be considered as a good indicator for it.
- The first-person video recording: subjects confessed that they were disturbed at the beginning of their activity and intended to show their best performance because of the recording device. However, they added that they very soon forgot about the subcam when involved in the nitty-gritty of the activity. In addition, should they have forced themselves to try to do their best, the bias would probably be negligible when related to the objective of the work analysis: accessing what makes competencies of workers, the best way to obtain exhaustive results is to observe experienced workers doing their best. Therefore, the bias induced by the first-perspective video is difficult to assess as it combines positive and negative contributions.

Is the method specialized?
To date, the method was here applied to occupational activities at a nuclear power plant and medicine (see Chapter 5), and at school in the framework of a pilot study. The context of occupational activities was that of high-risk industries where activities are mainly based on technical acts in the field. The professions analysed were technical. What about the activities of an assistant or a manager? Our conviction is that applying the method in these sorts of professions should pose no problem: the SPEAC model was developed on the basis of 50 different professions (see Chapter 3) of which 40% were managerial and 20% tertiary. These professions contributed towards validating the four-pole pattern of the model. Similarly, the four-pole model must be able to provide relevant output matrixes for these professions. The results obtained during the pilot study at school confirm this assumption.

The SEBE/SPEAC protocol and the delayed interview
Might the delay between the activity performance and the replay interview (RIW) have any influence on the collected information after the RIW?
Correlation coefficients calculated between these delays and the results obtained were low and not significant ($r=0.23$, $p>0.23$) and no particular tendency was identified. The average value for the delay was (in hours) $M=59.1$ with $SD=39.6$.

Therefore, we may conclude that our current data has shown that the delay between the activity performance and the replay interview could last 4 days without disturbing the method efficacy. However, we did not test the effect of what the subjects might experience during these 4 days: a traumatic accident, for example, might change the results.

4.5 Risk Assessment When Applying SEBE Methods

Despite the fact that applications of SEBE methods might induce additional risks in an industrial context by interacting with the equipment or disturbing workers, no suggestions regarding these concerns and no solutions helping researchers or work analysts to anticipate this kind of risks were available in the literature until the work undertaken with the SEBE-Lab of the LSE (UK) in collaboration with the Laboratory for Research in Sciences of Energy (France) and Electricité de France. We developed and tested a protocol for risk assessment when applying a

SEBE method (including eye-tracking methods) with a hundred participants and seven different professions (see open access articles: Fauquet-Alekhine, 2016b; Fauquet-Alekhine et al., 2018). The elaborated protocol gave satisfactory results in terms of risk prevention and time application: no incident or accident occurred and the risk assessment took less than 5 min.

The risk assessment protocol, applicable to any kind of SEBEmethods, is available in pdf format for free online at: http://hayka-kultura.org/larsen.html or http://www.sebe-lab.net with an associated tutorial video.

4.6 For Further Application

On the basis of the SPEAC model combined with a psychodynamic approach, a method was developed and applied in a French company for psychosocial risk assessment regarding 35 professions and focusing on difficulties related to skill discretion: Fauquet-Alekhine and Rouillac (2016) depicted and analysed four cases illustrating this; in addition, the insight of the in-depth analysis for one profession and a macro-approach taking all the professions into account were considered. Beyond the characterization of the psychosocial risks and the orientation regarding remedial measures implemented, the method enabled Fauquet-Alekhine and Rouillac to objectify and quantify the risks and helped them to centre the remedial measures on the right target or to better assess the degree of emergency of remedial measures. The results also showed that the method is exhaustive for psychosocial risk assessment provided that it is combined with other tools.

References

Andrén, M., Sanne, J. M., & Linel, P. (2010). Striking the balance between formality and informality in safety-critical communication: Train traffic control calls. *Journal of Pragmatics, 42*, 220–241.

Bentley, T., Johnston, L., & Baggo, K. V. (2005). *Evaluation using cued-recall debrief to elicit information about a user's affective experiences. In Citizens Online: Considerations for Today and the Future.* OZCHI '05 Proceedings of the 17th Australia Conference on Computer–Human Interaction for the Computer–Human Interaction Special Interest Group (CHISIG) of Australia, Narrabundah, Australia.

Bogusławski, A. (1994). Non-literal interpretation, metaphor, analogical proportion. *Word matters*, 137–155.

Cameron, A. F., & Webster, J. (2005). Unintended consequences of emerging communication technologies: Instant messaging in the workplace. *Computers in Human Behavior, 21*, 85–103.

Clot, Y. (1999). *La fonction psychologique du travail*. Paris: Ed. PUF.

Clot, Y., Faïta, D., Fernandez, G., & Scheller, L. (2001). Entretiens en auto-confrontation croisée: une méthode en clinique de l'activité. *Education Permanente, 146*(1), 17–25.

Coolican, H. (2009). *Research methods and statistics in psychology*. London: Hodder Arnold.

Crane, J., & Hannibal, J. (2009). *Psychology*. Oxford: Oxford University Press.

Denning, S. (2004). Telling Tales. *Harvard Business Review*.

Durand, J. P. (2001). Filmer le social? *L'Homme et La Société, 4*(142), 27–44.

Engelkamp, J., & Cohen, R. L. (1991). Current issues in memory of action events. *Psychological Research, 53*(3), 175–182.

Engeström, Y. (1987). *Learning by expanding: An activity-theoretical approach to developmental research*. Helsinki: Orienta-Konsultit.

Engeström, Y. (2006). Activity theory and expansive design. In S. Bagnara & G. Crampton Smith (Eds.), *Theories and practice of interaction design* (pp. 3–23). Mahwah, NJ: Erlbaum.

Engeström, Y., & Sannino, A. (2010). Studies of expansive learning: Foundations, findings and future challenges. *Educational Research Review, 5*, 1–24.

Erden, Z., von Krogh, G., & Nonaka, I. (2008). The quality of group tacit knowledge. *The Journal of Strategic Information Systems, 17*(1), 4–18.

Falzon, P. (1994). Les activités méta-fonctionnelles et leur assistance. *Le Travail Humain, 57*(1), 1–23.

Falzon, P. (1997). Travail et vidéo. In A. Borzeix, M. Lacoste, P. Falzon, M. Grosjean, & D. Cru (Eds.), *Filmer le travail: recherche et réalisation: Champs visuels n°6*. Paris: L'Harmattan.

Fauquet, Ph. (2006). *Pilotage et Coopération en salle de commande - Observations & analyse*. EDF Report reference D.5170/DIR/NED/06.002.

Fauquet-Alekhine, Ph. (2009). Надежность рабочего сообщения для операторов ядерных реакторов: изучение на тренажерах, анализ случаев и укрепление безопасности [Reliability of operational communication for pilots of nuclear reactors: Studies on simulators, events analysis, and reinforcement of safety]. Presented at the *XXXIIe Coll. Int. De Linguistique Fonctionnelles*, Minsk, 7–10 octobre 2009. Printed in *Prosodie, Traduction, Fonction*, L. Morozova & E. Weider (Eds.), Bruxelles: EME, 2011 (pp. 207–210).

Fauquet-Alekhine, Ph. (2010). *Use of simulator training for the study of operational communication—The case of pilots of French nuclear reactors:*

Reinforcement of reliability. Presented at the International Conference on Simulation Technology for Power Plants, San Diego, USA, February 2010. Published in Annual Simulation Symposium (ANSS 2010, New-York: Red Hook), 43, pp. 216–221.

Fauquet-Alekhine, Ph. (2012). Safety and reliability for nuclear production. *Socio-organizational Factors for Safe Nuclear Operation, 1*, 25–30.

Fauquet-Alekhine, Ph. (2013). *Expérimentation sur Stage Conduite Lignage (CLIG) / Simulateur de Pilotage UFPI Chinon*. Activity Report. Internal Work Document Reference RAC 2013-25 ind00, Appendix 1.

Fauquet-Alekhine, Ph. (2016a). Subjective ethnographic protocol for work activity analysis and occupational training improvement. *British Journal of Applied Science & Technology, 12*(5), 1–16. Article No. BJAST.21632.

Fauquet-Alekhine, Ph. (2016b). Risk assessment for subjective evidence-based ethnography applied in high risk environment. *Advances in Research, 6*(2), 1–13. Article No. AIR.21597.

Fauquet-Alekhine, Ph. (2017a). Psycholinguistic analysis of operational communication (Part I): The standard usage of communication in high risk industries. *Linguistics Journal, 12*(1), 86–109.

Fauquet-Alekhine, Ph. (2017b). Psycholinguistic analysis of operational communication (Part II): Prescribed communication for reliability in high risk industries. *European Journal of Language Studies, 4*(2), 27–40.

Fauquet-Alekhine, Ph. (2020). *Metaphor as a powerful tool for activity analysis: Detection, selection and application*. Communication and Language at Work (submitted to).

Fauquet-Alekhine, Ph., & Boucherand, A. (2011). *Analyse Socio-Organisationnelle & Humaine: étude des causes profondes – Chinon 2010–2011*. EDF Internal Report ref: D.5170/DIR/NED/11.005.

Fauquet-Alekhine, Ph., & Boucherand, A. (2012). The structuring effects of tools in risky industrial work activity: Failures and solutions. *Socio-organizational Factors for Safe Nuclear Operation, 1*, 63–67.

Fauquet-Alekhine, Ph., & Boucherand, A. (2015). The structuring effect of tools conceptualized through the initial goal fixedness for work activity. *Cognition, Technology & Work, 18*(1), 145–160.

Fauquet-Alekhine, Ph., & Daviet, Fr. (2015). Detection and characterization of tacit occupational knowledge through speech and behavior analysis. *International Journal of Innovation, Management and Technology, 6*(1), 21–25.

Fauquet-Alekhine, Ph., & Maridonneau, C. (2016). Piloting nuclear reactors, In Ph. Fauquet-Alekhine & N. Pehuet (Eds.), *Simulation & training: Fundamentals and Applications* (pp. 59–86). Berlin: Springer Verlag.

Fauquet-Alekhine, Ph., & Martinez, P. (2020). Cognitive task analysis to improve student competencies: A pilot study based on the use of the Square of PErceived ACtion model. *Teachers & Teaching* (submitted to).

Fauquet-Alekhine, Ph., & Rouillac, L. (2016). The square of perceived action model as a tool for identification, prevention and treatment of factors deteriorating mental health at work, *Journal of Mental Disorder & Treatment, 2*(3), Paper #1000126.

Fauquet-Alekhine, Ph., & Lahlou, S. (2017). The Square of PErceived ACtion model (SPEAC model) applied in digital ethnography for work activity analysis: Performance and workers' perception. *Current Journal of Applied Science & Technology, 22*(3): 1–13. Article No. CJAST.34985.

Fauquet-Alekhine Ph., & Lahlou, S. (2020). Performance in collaborative activity: contribution of Intersubjectivity Theory. *Cognition, Work & Technology* (submitted to).

Fauquet-Alekhine, Ph., Le Bellu, S., Buchet, M., Berton, J., Bouhours, G., Daviet, Fr., … Lahlou, S. (2018). Risk assessment for subjective evidence-based ethnography applied in high risk environment: Improved protocol. *Advances in Research, 16*(3), 1–15. Article No. AIR.43259.

Garcia-Lorenzo, L. (2010). Framing uncertainty: Narratives, change and digital technologies. *Social Science Information, 49*(3), 329–350.

Gillespie, A., & Richardson, B. (2011). Exchanging social positions: Enhancing perspective-taking within a cooperative problem solving task. *European Journal of Social Psychology, 41*, 608–616.

Glucksberg, S. (2003). The psycholinguistics of metaphor. *Trends in Cognitive Sciences, 7*(2), 92–96.

Goddard, C. (2004). The ethnopragmatics and semantics of 'active metaphors'. *Journal of Pragmatics, 36*(7), 1211–1230.

Goldman, R., Pea, R., Barron, B., & Derry, S. (2007). *Video research in the learning sciences.* Mahwah, NJ: Lawrence Erlbaum Associates.

Gordon, S. E., Schmierer, K. A., & Gill, R. T. (1993). Conceptual graph analysis: Knowledge acquisition for instructional systems design. *Human Factors, 35*, 459–481.

Heath, C., & Hindmarsh, J. (2002). Analysing interaction: Video, ethnography and situated conduct. *Qualitative Research in Action*, 99–121.

IAEA. (1998). *Experience in the use of systematic approach to training (SAT) for nuclear power plant personnel.* Report Reference IAEA-TECDOC-1057. International Atomic Energy Agency, Vienna (Austria).

Knoblauch, H., Schnettler, B., Raab, J., & Soeffner, H. G. (2006). *Video-analysis methodology and methods: Qualitative audiovisual data analysis in sociology.* Frankfurt am Main, Berlin, Bern, Bruxelles, New York, Oxford, and Wien: Peter Lang.

Krauss, R. M., & Fussell, S. R. (1989). Mutual knowledge and communicative effectiveness. In R. E. Kraut, J. Gallegher, & C. Egido (Eds.), *Intellectual teamwork: Social and technical bases of collaborative work.* New York: Erlbaum.

Krauss, R. M., & Weinheimer, S. (1967). Effect of referent similarity and communication mode on verbal encoding. *Journal of Verbal Learning and Verbal Behavior, 6*(3), 359–363.

Lahlou, S. (1999). Observing cognitive work in offices. In N. Streitz, J. Siegel, V. Hartkopf, & S. Konomi (Eds.), *Cooperative buildings: Integrating information, organizations and architecture* (Vol. 1670, pp. 150–163). Heidelberg: Springer, Lecture Notes in Computer Science.

Lahlou, S. (2006). L'activité du point de vue de l'acteur et la question de l'inter-subjectivité: huit années d'expériences avec des caméras miniaturisées fixées au front des acteurs (subcam). *Communications, 80,* 209–234.

Lahlou, S. (2011). How we can capture the subject's perspective? An evidence-based approach for the social scientist. *Social Science Information, 50*(3–4), 607–655.

Lahlou, S., Le Bellu, S., & Boesen-Mariani, S. (2015). Subjective evidence based ethnography: method and applications. *Integrative Psychological and Behavioral Science, 49*(2), 216–238.

Lakoff, G. (1993). The contemporary theory of metaphor. *Metaphor and Thought, 2,* 202–251.

Lakoff, G., & Johnson, M. (1980a). The metaphorical structure of the human conceptual system. *Cognitive Science, 4*(2), 195–208.

Lakoff, G., & Johnson, M. (1980b). Conceptual metaphor in everyday language. *The Journal of Philosophy*, 453–486.

Lakoff, G., & Johnson, M. (1980/2003). *Metaphors we live by.* Chicago: University of Chicago.

Le Bellu, S. (2011). *Capitalisation des savoir-faire et des gestes professionnels dans le milieu industriel* (PhD thesis). University of Bordeau, Reference 2011BOR21825.

Le Bellu, S. (2016). Learning the secrets of the craft through the real-time experience of experts: Capturing and transferring experts' tacit knowledge to novices. *PISTES*, 18-1, http://pistes.revues.org/4685.

Le Bellu, S., Lahlou, S., & Nosulenko, V. (2010). Capter et transférer le savoir incorporé dans un geste professionnel. *Social Science Information, 49,* 371–413.

Leplat, J. (2000). *L'analyse psychologique de l'activité en ergonomie. Aperçu sur son évolution, ses modèles et ses méthodes.* Toulouse: Octares.

Limaye, M. (1992). Conceptual and methodological issues in organizational communication research: A comment on "categorizing professional discourse". *Journal of Business and Technical Communication, 6,* 488–490.

Luff, P., & Heath, Ch. D. (2012). Some 'technical challenges' of video analysis: Social actions, objects, material realities and the problems of perspective. *Qualitative Research, 12*(3), 255–279.

Luff, P., Jirotka, M., Yamashita, N., Kuzuoka, H., Heath, Ch., & Eden, G. (2013). Embedded interaction: The accomplishment of actions in everyday and video-mediated environments. *ACM Transactions on Computer-Human Interaction, 20*(1), 6.1–6.22.

Mollo, V., & Falzon, P. (2004). Auto- and allo-confrontation as tools for reflective activities. *Applied Ergonomics, 35,* 331–540.

Oddone, I., Re, A., & Briante, G. (1981). *Redécouvrir l'expérience ouvrière: vers une autre psychologie du travail?* Paris: Editions Sociales.

Omodei, M. M., & McLennan, J. (1994). Studying complex decision making in natural settings: Using a head mounted video camera to study competitive orienteering. *Perceptual and Motor Skills, 79,* 1411–1425.

Omodei, M. M., McLennan, J., & Wearing, J. W. (2005). How expertise is applied in real-world dynamic environments: Head-mounted video and cued recall as a methodology for studying routines of decision making. In T. Betsch & S. Haberstroh (Eds.), *The routines of decision making*. Mahwah, NJ: Lawrence Erlbaum Associates.

Pea, R. D. (1994). Seeing what we build together: Distributed multimedia learning environments for transformative communications. *Journal of the Learning Sciences, 3*(3), 285–299.

Petitmengin, C. (2009). The validity of first-person descriptions as authenticity and coherence. *Journal of Consciousness Studies, 16*(10–12), 252–284.

Polanyi, M. (1967). *The tacit dimension*. New York: Anchor Books.

Rieken, J., Garcia-Sanchez, E., Trujillo, M. P., & Bear, D. (2015). Digital ethnography and the social dimension of introspection: An empirical study in two Colombian schools. *Integrative Psychological and Behavioral Science, 49*(2), 253–274.

Rix, G., & Biache, M. (2004). Enregistrement en perspective subjective située et entretien en re situ subjectif: une méthodologie de constitution de l'expérience. *Intellectica, 1*(38), 363–396.

Rix-Lièvre, G., & Lièvre, P. (2010). An innovative observatory of polar expedition projects: An investigation of organizing. *Project Management Journal, 41*(3), 91–98.

Roth, W. M. (2004). Perceptual gestalts in workplace communication. *Journal of Pragmatics, 36,* 1037–1069.

Smythies, J. (1996). A note on the concept of the visual field in neurology, psychology, and visual neuroscience. *Perception, 25*(3), 369–371.

Steen, G. J. (2011). The contemporary theory of metaphor—Now new and improved! *Review of Cognitive Linguistics, 9*(1), 26–64.

Theureau, J. (2002, November 12–15). *L'entretien d'autoconfrontation comme composante d'un programme de recherche empirique & technologique*. Paper presented at the IIème Journées Internationales des Sciences du Sport, Paris.

Tofel-Grehl, C., & Feldon, D. F. (2013). Cognitive task analysis-based training: A meta-analysis of studies. *Journal of Cognitive Engineering and Decision Making, 7*(3), 293–304.

Tulving, E. (1972). Episodic and semantic memory. In D. E. T. W. (Ed.), *Organization of memory* (pp. 381–403). New York: Academic Press.

Tulving, E. (2002). Episodic memory: From mind to brain. *Annual Review of Psychology, 53,* 1–25.

Veraksa, A. N. (2013). Symbol as a cognitive tool. *Psychology in Russia: State of the Art, 1,* 57–65.

Vermersch, P. (1994/2006). *L'entretien d'explicitation.* Issy-les-Moulineaux: ESF Editeur.

Von Cranach, M., Kalbermatten, U., Indermühle, K., & Gugler, B. (1982). *Goal-directed action.* London: Academic Press.

Wasonga, T. A., & Murphy, J. F. (2006). Learning from tacit knowledge: The impact of the internship. *International Journal of Educational Management, 20*(2), 153–163.

Wei, J., & Salvendy, G. (2000). Development of the purdue cognitive job analysis methodology. *International Journal of Cognitive Ergonomics, 4*(4), 277–296.

Wei, J., & Salvendy, G. (2004). The cognitive task analysis methods for job and task design: Review and reappraisal. *Behaviour & Information Technology, 23*(4), 273–299.

Wickström, G., & Bendix, T. (2000). The Hawthorne effect—What did the original Hawthorne studies actually show? *Scandinavian Journal of Work, Environment & Health,* 363–367.

CHAPTER 5

Application of the SEBE/SPEAC Protocol

Abstract This chapter gives three examples of application of the SEBE/SPEAC protocol, one regarding activities related to reliability practices for professionals of nuclear industries, another about a simple nursing activity in medicine, the radial puncture and a last one in education at school. Results in terms of consecutive operational performances are presented to illustrate the efficiency of the protocol. The acceptance of the protocol by workers is also analysed and discussed, yielding a data-based demonstration showing that the protocol is well accepted by participants.

Keywords SEBE/SPEAC protocol · Application · Occupational training

5.1 Reliable Practices in Nuclear Industry

Nuclear production consists in producing electric energy from nuclear energy. If the basic idea is quite simple, the implementation gives complex socio-technical systems that imply strict rules and requirements to guaranty the safety of the industrial plants and of course of the people working there or living around. With the aim to ensure nuclear safety, a high level of reliability is expected from the teams when performing their work activities.

In the perspective of a sustained improvement, an international benchmark addressing reliability in high-risk industries (different countries, different industries) was undertaken by experts of EDF SA

P. Fauquet-Alekhine, *Knowledge Management in High Risk Industries*, https://doi.org/10.1007/978-3-030-49213-7_5

in the early 2000s. This was carried out to identify especially: (i) how a safe industry can progress by avoiding minor events (i.e. deviation from the expected result)? (ii) what helps a worker to avoid minor events? A Human Performance Program resulted from this benchmark within the framework of which an area for improvement addressed the reliability of the workers while performing their activities (see details and related studies in Fauquet-Alekhine, 2012, 2017a, 2017b). Six practices became mandatory for any worker acting on the industrial process:

- Pre-job briefing: takes place after the preparation of activity, a specific phase of mental preparation and coordination for the people taking part in the intervention.
- The "Take a Minute": takes place in the workplace and just before it starts, it requires workers to analyse the work environment.
- Self-check: involves sequential reading of the procedure identity tag and its corresponding tag on the equipment before the implementation of an action.
- Peer-check: another person verifies the agreement between the intention announced and the draft of the forthcoming action.
- Activity debriefing: at the end of the activity, it raises the positive and negative aspects of the activity.
- Reliable communication or 3-way communication: to ensure that information has reached the consciousness of the person doing the intervention by repeating information received and confirming it.

These practices were said "reliability practices" or "human performance tools" (HP tools). From 2006 to 2009, all the staff in maintenance and operations departments were trained to understand and apply these practices and then had a refresher training every two years. Significant improvements were observed during the first years following the beginning of the implementation of the programme, but the progress came to stagnate after 2012.

After several socio-organizational analyses, the management of the French Chinon nuclear power plant (Chinon NPP) made the assumption that the six reliability practices might not be correctly performed especially due to the renewal of the staff. It was thus decided to apply the SEBE/SPEAC protocol to obtain a refined description of competencies needed to apply the reliability practices and to use this information as input data for a new training session addressing reliability practices in the Operation shift teams. This was initiated mid-2014.

The SEBE/SPEAC protocol was thus applied during the simulated situations (SimS) for an activity performed by a "role-model", a person identified as having a high level of mastering for reliability practices. This person signed an informed consent for video recording (see, example in Appendix). Ethical approval (Code of Approval: DSP/RS/PFA-4) for the study was obtained from the Ethics Committee of the Department of Social Psychology (LSE, London, UK). The results of this activity analysis, a matrix giving knowledge and know-how per fields of competencies, were used to develop the content and the pedagogical objectives of the simulation training sessions.

The resulting training sessions summoned about 60% of the staff of the Operations teams during one year in 2015. A change of performance in safety and/or production was then observed in 2016 and 2017 with a significant decrease of about 30% per year in terms of insufficient quality associated with a lack of compliance with reliability practices. The management goal was achieved. At the same time, costs avoided through the quality improvement were estimated in tens of k€ (Fauquet-Alekhine, 2017d, 2019). Finally, the demonstration of the effectiveness of the SEBE/SPEAC protocol to provide relevant input data for training programmes was reinforced.

In addition, the performance of the method was assessed by an external entity: in November 2016, the WANO[1] peer reviewers spent two weeks at Chinon NPP checking in depth the process and the organization performances. They identified areas for improvement and strengths. Among the latter, the new training programme for Reliability Practices in Operations teams was awarded: this work was identified as demonstrating "a new, higher level of excellence that would benefit other plants in the industry to emulate [...] [and] should be considered as 'redefining' excellence" with a possibility to "likely drive change in the industry". In 2017, WANO asked Chinon NPP to provide a short description of the method in order to broadcast it at an international level.

[1] WANO is the World Association of Nuclear Operators. It gathers all industries worldwide providing electricity from nuclear energy. WANO undertakes periodically peer reviews in NPPs with the help of internationally renowned experts. WANO's assessment is always the reference.

After this first success, applications of the SEBE/SPEAC protocol were used to improve training sessions for other activities, individual and collective. It was also applied with the aim to provide relevant short pedagogical videos for experts to reactivate their competencies just before performing a complex and/or rare and/or sensitive activity in real operating situations (ROS) (Fauquet-Alekhine, 2017c; Fauquet-Alekhine & Lahlou, 2017).

5.2 Radial Puncture in Medicine

The head manager of the Medical Training Centre of Angers (France) was told of the possibility to apply the SEBE/SPEAC protocol at the end of 2015 (Fauquet-Alekhine & Daviet, 2015) and showed a frank interest after the results obtained in nuclear industry. The head manager identified very soon an activity for which the trainers had difficulties to make trainees improving their professional practices: the radial puncture aiming at providing a sample of blood for arterial blood gas (ABG) test. This test measures the amounts of certain gases (e.g. CO_2, O_2) dissolved in arterial blood. The radial puncture (individual activity) consists in puncturing an artery with a needle and syringe in order to obtain a small sample of blood, the most common puncture site being the radial artery at the wrist (Fig. 5.1).

During the university year, groups of medical students are summoned to the Training Centre of Angers (France) to be trained on part-task

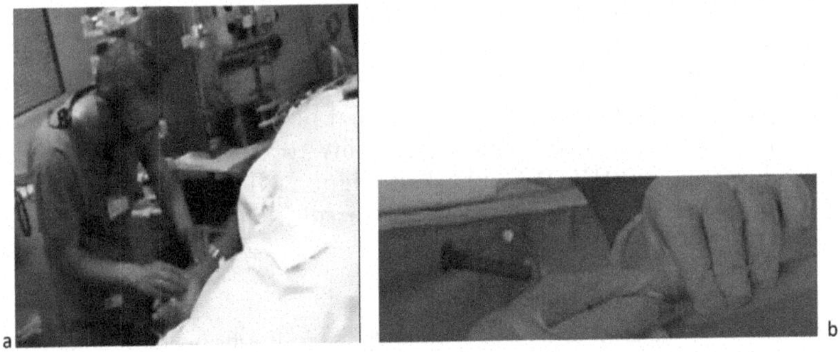

Fig. 5.1 Radial puncture for arterial blood gas (ABG) test: **a** in context. **b** on the wrist

simulators reproducing the arm-wrist-hand segment complete with blood circulation. The work activity is individual as shown in Fig. 5.1a. The activity could be easily implemented in two sessions, each gathering 12 subjects, the first one having a "classic form" (what they were used to doing at the Medical Training Centre) and the second adjusted using data provided after applying the SEBE/SPEAC protocol.

The SEBE/SPEAC protocol was applied to a reference situation in ROS in June 2016: a volunteer experienced anaesthetist signed the informed consent form and scheduled a one-hour slot to record a film of the activity after applying the risk assessment protocol (see Sect. 4.5 "Risk Assessment When Applying SEBE Methods" in Chapter 4) and another 2-hour slot for validation of the data. The hospital management dealt with agreements for video recording. Ethical approval (Code of Approval: DSP/RS/PFA-4) for the study was obtained from the Ethics Committee of the Department of Social Psychology (LSE, London, UK).

A half-day meeting was then planned to analyse the results. The outcome matrix was used to rethink the content of the training sessions and to elaborate a new assessment grid of the residents' performance at the end of the simulation training sessions.

The two sessions were compared in terms of residents' performance: the classic session (as it was carried out before using the results provided by SEBE/SPEAC analysis) and the restructured session (carried out when integrating the results provided by SEBE/SPEAC analysis). Results showed a significant improvement in the performance of the restructured session when compared with the classic session:

- The average score of the participants sample increased by more than 13% ($t(\mathrm{df}=21)=3.98$; $p<0.001$ for a t-test).
- The standard deviation was more than halved.
- The percentage of trainees whose score was over 90% of the maximum score was multiplied by more than 5.

It is important to note that all that was achieved with 100% success in the classic session was kept at this level in the restructured session and the other assessment items were increased from the classic to the restructured session. Results are presented and discussed in Fauquet-Alekhine et al. (2020).

The performance in real operating situations was not assessed. The reason for this was that students came to the Training Centre from different parts of the region and the assessment would have implied an enormous amount of time spent on the road for a medical expert to be able to carry out the assessments. It could also have been undertaken by a local expert but experience has shown that such experts are not available for this sort of task most of the time and, a fortiori, not available at the moment the radial puncture is performed and may be assessed.

After this first test, applications of the SEBE/SPEAC protocol are envisaged for a complex activity for which performance assessment in ROS can be possible.

5.3 Economics and Social Science at School

Having developed protocol, tested and applied the SEBE/SPEAC in occupational area, the question was raised as to its possible application in an educational context. The purpose of applying the protocol at school was to assess whether it could help students to improve their skills for a task identified as difficult and for which current lessons did not provide sufficient progress. A pilot study was carried out at Saint-Louis School (Institution Saint-Louis, Saumur, France) with students in secondary education (2 years before joining university) with two classes (one for the control-group, the other for the test-group) specializing in economics and social science.

The design of the pilot study (Fig. 5.2) consisted in selecting a work activity (a short exercise) for which the teacher wanted to modify his

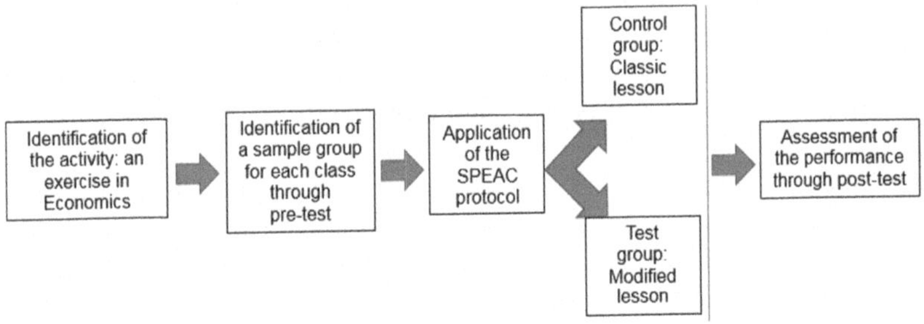

Fig. 5.2 Design of the pilot study addressing skills improvement at school

method of teaching in order to help the students progress more efficiently; a phase of analysis of the work activity and a teaching phase were preceded and followed-up by a pre-test and a post-test in order to assess the variation in students' performance.

The analysis of the activity was undertaken using the SEBE/SPEAC protocol. The selected activity consisted of a productivity analysis of an industry on the basis of a series of calculations which were carried out using data provided in a table. The teacher had chosen a skilled student volunteer to perform the activity. After presenting the experiment to the student and her parents and then signing an informed consent. Ethical approval (Code of Approval: LRN-DHS/19/01) for the study was obtained from the Ethics Committee of the Department of Human Science (German branch of the Lab. for Research in Sciences of Energy, Munich, Germany). The student individually completed the activity with a miniature camera mounted on her spectacles so as to record the performance from a first-person perspective (subjective view of the action). The recording was then visualized in the presence of the student, the teacher and the researcher (this interview was also video-recorded) so as to question the student about what had been done, complying with the SEBE/SPEAC protocol. After the interview, the researcher elaborated a matrix of competencies for the activity. Before this phase of the experiment, the researcher interviewed the teacher with the same objective: to elaborate a matrix of competencies from the point of view of the teacher for the selected activity. We hypothesized that the comparative analysis of the two matrices would make it possible to identify differences (the student's matrix was expected to be more complete than that of the teacher) allowing us to adjust the teaching of the activity and to improve the students' performance afterwards.

The pre- and post-tests were written exams with an exercise of the same type as that of the chosen activity but of different content. Between the two written tests, the control-group attended a classic lesson in that the lesson did not benefit from the results of the SEBE/SPEAC analysis. The test-group, on the other hand, followed a lesson benefiting from these contributions. The pre- and post-tests were marked according to a pre-defined evaluation grid, comprised of 22 criteria each scoring 1 point. This ensured an objective quantified evaluation of the subjects' performance. Between the two tests, the subjects did not have access to the copies of the first test and were not aware of their score. The tests were carried out under identical working conditions.

The two sample groups of students (control-group and test-group) were made up of 18 students (mean age: 17 years old) from each 30-student class. They were selected so that the annual average performances of each group as well as the average performances at the pre-test were similar (validated through t-test of Student and χ^2).

The results showed that:

- The matrix of competencies from the student was indeed more complete than that of the teacher.
- The improvement in the test-group between the pre- and post-tests was significant (+46% in score, $p=0.002$) conversely for the control-group.
- The average score for the test-group was significantly higher than that of the control-group for the post-test (+23%, $p<0.05$).

The pilot study thus demonstrated the applicability of the SEBE/SPEAC protocol in the educational space and showed the benefits for teaching, helping to make it more relevant, more comprehensive, as well as integrating tacit and non-specific skills (which can also apply to other exercises). The results were presented at the conference "Social psychology and society: history and modernity", Moscow State University of Psychology & Education (Фоке-Алехин & Мартинес, 2019). They gave rise to further applications of the SPEAC protocol at school with articles in English (Fauquet-Alekhine & Martinez, 2020) and prepared for French national educational publications to share this method.

5.4 Acceptance of the Protocol by Participants

The SPEAC protocol is not anodyne for the participants who have to wear additional video equipment during their work and then have to re-question their competencies with the researcher or the analyst. The question of the acceptance of the SEBE/SPEAC protocol by participants thus came up: the hypothesis was that participants would not appreciate being disturbed by the video equipment in the real operating field and that the replay interview would be perceived as an uncomfortable introspection and/or a disguised, unacknowledged assessment of their competencies.

Therefore, following each analysis, participants were presented with a 9-item questionnaire for self-assessment of the SEBE/SPEAC protocol answered on a Likert scale:

□ Strongly disagree □ Disagree □ Neither agree nor disagree □ Agree □ Strongly agree

Items addressed efficiency, constraints, extended application to colleagues or other activities:

1. Do you think that analysing the subjective film is a real added value compared to analysis without subjective film (i.e. a method said "classical")?
2. Do you think you progressed regarding this work activity with this method?
3. Do you think you progressed regarding the work activity faster when applying the method than with a so-called classical method?
4. Do you find the method (miniaturized camera and subjective film analysis) constraining for you?
5. Do you think the method is innovative?
6. Do you think the method is difficult to apply by analysts?
7. Do you think the method is worth to be applied to other work activities?
8. Do you think the method permits to highlight particularities which are invisible with a so-called classical method?
9. Do you think the method has any interest to be applied to your colleagues?

Assessing whether or not the SEBE/SPEAC protocol was well accepted by the participants could not be done from the two application examples described in the previous sections: for each example, the activity of only one professional was analysed and, although the two assessments were positive regarding the protocol, the statistical demonstration was not achieved. This is why we used here data from a series of activity analyses undertaken within another framework, this of the study of collaborative activities in Operations teams of a French nuclear power plant (Fauquet-Alekhine & Lahlou, 2020).

The SPEAC-based method was applied to analyse hydraulic configuration, Lock & Tag activities and periodical tests during real operating situations, each involving a pair of co-workers: pilot in the control room and a worker in the field. These activities were part of their routine work. The aim of the analyses was to provide the matrices of competencies necessary to perform each activity and use them later as input data for occupational training. As described in Chapter 4, the protocol implied a short preparation with the participants, a capture phase to obtain a first-person video recording of each co-worker's activity, then a RIW followed by an analysis by the analyst to identify knowledge and know-how necessary to perform the activity and a validation phase. As the analysis addressed a collaborative activity involving two co-workers, a collective RIW was also carried out before the validation phase.

The activities chosen for the study (hydraulic configuration, Lock & Tag activities and periodical tests) involved the two co-workers in a collaborative work implying respectively to change the equipment configuration used to carry fluids, lock pieces of equipment to ensure they are properly shut off and not started up again prior to the completion of maintenance or servicing work, and to perform sets of hydraulic and electric manipulations periodically undertaken by shift teams in order to test the reliability of the industrial process.

Over 8 weeks of shift, 15 situation cases (i.e. 30 participants) were observed and interviews were performed individually and then collectively with both co-workers. The capture phases usually took place during morning, afternoon or evening and RIW was undertaken by night during the next shift most of the time. After the validation phase, participants were presented with the 9-item questionnaire to assess the protocol.

Answers on the Likert scale were coded from −2 (strongly disagree) to +2 (strongly agree) and an average score was calculated for each question.

Analysis of the answers indicated that the participants' perception regarding the SEBE/SPEAC protocol was homogeneous with a good consistency: the Cronbach's alpha was $\alpha=0.75$ for the field workers and $\alpha=0.60$ for the pilots and $\alpha=0.66$ for the whole sample. Calculation of χ^2 showed that the pilots and field workers' distributions were similar: χ^2 $(1, \text{fd}=8)=0.76$, $p>0.5$.

In substance, the overall perception was positive. The average scores for each question for pilots, field workers and the whole sample are shown in Fig. 5.3.

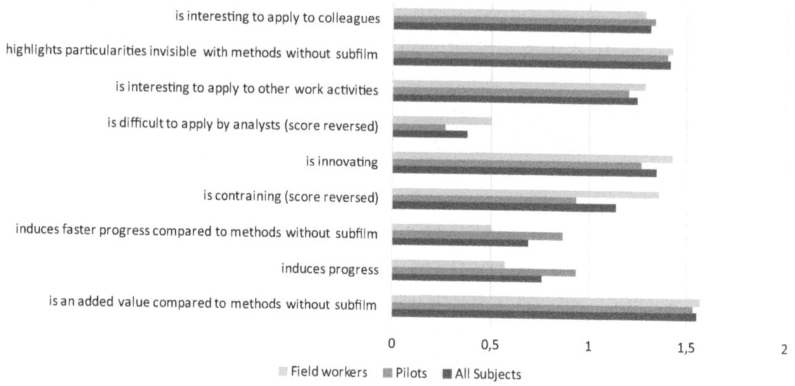

Fig. 5.3 Average scores for each question evaluating SEBE/SPEAC method used for analysing activities; assessment made by pilots and field workers

Overall:

- The protocol was perceived as an added value compared to a method without subjective film (i.e. a method said "classic"):
  mean score = 1.55 answers ticked 1 or more = 100%.
- The method induced faster progress than a "classical"method:
  mean score = 0.76 answers ticked 1 or more = 62%.
- The protocol was perceived not constraining, innovative, worth to be applied to other work activities:
  mean score = 1.24 answers ticked 1 or more = 89%.
- The protocol had interest to be applied to colleagues (as illustrated in Sect. 4.2.4.3 "Psychological Issues" in 4.2.4 "Subtleties of Application of the SEBE/SPEAC Protocol"):
  mean score = 1.31 answers ticked 1 or more = 96%.
  The method had interest to be applied to other work activities:
  mean score = 1.24 answers ticked 1 or more = 100%.

Although the questionnaire did not offer the possibility for the participants to explain the reasons of their answers, the participants' spontaneous comments at ends of RIW gave an insight of these reasons: they better understood what was done, they discovered bad habits like cutting off colleagues' speech, identified behaviours that should need corrections, were distantiated from the situation while viewing the sub-film thus providing a new standpoint; in addition to these personal benefits, it contributed to enhancing the collaborative work and helped them becoming aware of unconscious good practices.

The key information that provides the data from the questionnaire is that:

- Applying the SEBE/SPEAC protocol for work analysis is not just an analysis: answers show that it is also a lever of professional improvement for each participant as illustrated by their aforementioned spontaneous comments and confirmed by the mean score for questions addressing progress induced by the method. This was already reported in analogous studies (e.g. Le Bellu, 2016: 22).
- Participants will be good advertisers for the SEBE/SPEAC protocol as the overall perception was positive and because they found it interesting to apply to other activities as well as to colleagues.

We may also assume that the application of the SEBE/SPEAC protocol is perceived by the participants as a particular interest for their daily job, not only from the analyst but also from the management who usually sponsors the work analysis. This might be another positive point contributing to the participants' acceptance of the protocol.

From all these elements, we may conclude that, when there is a need to implement the SEBE/SPEAC protocol within the teams of a complex socio-technical system, managers and analysts must be confident regarding the acceptance of the protocol by the workers.

Parts of these results were published in Fauquet-Alekhine et al. (2020).

5.5 Further Applications

The following sections present a list of applications beyond the analysis of competencies in action. These examples illustrate the rich potential of the SPEAC model.

5.5.1 *Enhancement of Students' Teaching and Training*

The purpose of teachers at school or at university is to develop students' skills. Even if teaching begins with providing knowledge via lectures, the development of competencies is a goal (see the KKHS model in Chapter 2). Competencies are developed through tutorials, practical work, personal work exercises, training periods, for example. Putting competencies in action is therefore just as important for the students as for the workers. The SPEAC model may thus help teachers to improve teaching for those students whose results are insufficient or below expectations as illustrated in Chapter 4.

Another solution suggested is that teachers identify the activity which poses difficulty (by activity, it is necessary to understand, for example, a method of analysis of a text, a writing method, an exercise specific to the application of a mathematical formula), and then undertake a reflexive analysis of the competencies that are necessary for them to carry out this activity. Doing so, teachers obtain the associated matrix of competencies. The teachers then identify which K&KH are lacking for the students in this matrix by seeing things from the students' standpoint or exchanging with the students. Lastly, teachers analyse the possible dysfunctions (incoherence or inadequacy of poles in particular according to the static and dynamic approaches, see Chapter 3). Searching for the right balance of the SPEAC modelization of the activity makes it possible to improve teaching.

5.5.2 *Competencies and Well-Being at Work*

Subjects' mental health at work is intimately linked with their perception of well-being, itself associated with their perception of their competencies among other factors. Sheldon and Elliot (1999: 484) noted that "there are natural satisfactions to be found in the process of exercising one's competencies to move toward desired outcomes" (see also Judge, Bono, Erez, & Locke, 2005). All models aiming at describing mental health of workers include this aspect (see, for example, the reviews of Mark & Smith, 2008; Nieuwenhuijsen, Bruinvels, & Frings-Dresen, 2010).

Consequently, increasing a positive perception of competencies contributes to improving mental health: Mann, Hosman, Schaalma, and De Vries, (2004: 359), for instance, noted how self-perceived competence could contribute to enhance self-esteem, thus suggesting the contribution of perceived competencies to mental health promotion indirectly through self-esteem.

Several studies were carried out to define how perceived competence could be characterized at work (see, for example, Ankudinov, Lebedev, & Sachenkov, 2015; Bentley, Kavanagh, Krnjacki, & La Montagne, 2015; Bowling, Eschleman, & Wang, 2010; Joensuu et al., 2010;

Karasek, 1979; Mann et al. 2004; Oomens, Geurts, & Scheepers, 2007; Ryan, 1995; Sheldon & Elliot, 1999). Four criteria have been adopted by a large part of the scientific community: the level of skill, the repetitive nature of tasks and the possibility to learn new things or to develop special abilities or to be creative. In an early work, Karasek (1979) designated these criteria under the concept of "skill discretion".

These considerations highlight the direct and indirect contribution of perceived competencies to the subjective well-being at work. Consequently, any method permitting to identify what could make the subjects' perception of competencies positive or negative might contribute to improve mental health at work.

In this perspective, the Square of PErceived ACtion model (SPEAC model) helps practitioners and researchers for identification of strengths and weaknesses affecting mental health at work when related to skill discretion.

The model was used in this aim and applied to different situations in the frame of psychosocial risk assessment and showed interesting results (Fauquet-Alekhine & Rouillac, 2016): fast, objective and determinant identification of psychosocial risks and associated remedial measures when related to skill discretion were obtained.

5.5.3 Industrial Event Analysis

Industrial event analysis designates the analysis undertaken in an industrial company to understand how an event (a deviation from what was expected) could occur: technical, socio-organizational and human factors are therefore considered and remedial solutions are identified in order to avoid such problems recurring.

It happens that workers' competencies are identified among these factors.

To understand how the optimal use of competencies has been difficult, the conditions needed to carry out the activity can be analysed using the SPEAC model.

The model argues that competencies are successfully put in action when the four poles of the SPEAC model respect the properties of efficiency and adequacy according to two approaches: static and dynamic.

The static approach is to consider that "putting competencies successfully in action" is achieved when all four poles are effective, i.e. "available" and "coherent". "Available" means that the content of a pole is defined and actually exists for the subject to act. "Coherent" means that any part of a pole does not counter another part of the same pole.

Example: the pole *Having to act* is not available if a procedure is missing and is not consistent if you have to do a job in less time than is possible.

The dynamic approach of the model considers interpolar relationships. Each of them must account for the symmetrical adequacy between the poles. Any mismatch between several poles can lead to conflict between these poles, which can lead to difficulties in putting competencies successfully in action.

Example: the poles *Having to act* and *Being able to act* are not in adequacy if you have to write but there is no pen, no pencil.

This dynamic approach (and therefore the property of "adequacy") is added to the static approach (properties of "availability" and "coherence").

The use of the SPEAC model therefore consists in conducting an analysis addressing the coherence and the adequacy of the poles.

Thus, the SPEAC model is an effective tool to analyse the factor "competencies" in safety events and build appropriate solutions.

5.6 Who May Apply the SEBE/SPEAC Protocol?

Applying the SEBE/SPEAC protocol or using the SPEAC model is easy for any work analyst provided that competencies for interviews (individual and collective) have been elaborated beforehand. This is the cases of many psychologists, sociologists or ergonomists.

The protocol is not very different from what is commonly applied by analysts; the main point is to integrate the SPEAC model in the analysis. Side points address the use of video equipment and the use of video recording during the interview. In case of difficulty, a training programme for self-confrontation and explicitation interview might be useful.

References

Ankudinov, A. B., Lebedev, O. V., & Sachenkov, A. A. (2015). Empirical analysis of job satisfaction determinants in Russia. *Asian Social Science, 11*(4), 117.

Baudo, G. (2015). Giogio Armani's staying power. *System Magazine, 5*, 38–51.

Bentley, R. J., Kavanagh, A., Krnjacki, L., & La Montagne, A. D. (2015). A longitudinal analysis of changes in job control and mental health. *American Journal of Epidemiology, 182*(4), 328–334.

Bowling, N. A., Eschleman, K. J., & Wang, Q. (2010). A meta-analytic examination of the relationship between job satisfaction and subjective well-being. *Journal of Occupational and Organizational Psychology, 83*(4), 915–934.

Fauquet-Alekhine, Ph. (2012). Safety and reliability for nuclear production. *Socio-Organizational Factors for Safe Nuclear Operation, 1*, 25–30.

Fauquet-Alekhine, Ph. (2017a). Psycholinguistic analysis of operational communication (Part I): The standard usage of communication in high risk industries. *Linguistics Journal, 12*(1), 86–109.

Fauquet-Alekhine, Ph. (2017b). Psycholinguistic analysis of operational communication (Part II): Prescribed communication for reliability in high risk industries. *European Journal of Language Studies, 4*(2), 27–40.

Fauquet-Alekhine, Ph. (2017c). *Method for developing a pre-activity video—Removal of RPR inhibitions* (EDF SA Internal Report Reference: D5170/DIR/NED/17.012).

Fauquet-Alekhine, Ph. (2017d). *Methodological & economic results regarding innovations for simulation training and professional performance developed with the LSE—2013–2017* (EDF SA Internal Report Reference: D5170/DIR/NED/17.008).

Fauquet-Alekhine, Ph. (2019, October 8–10). Financial stakes and simulation training. In *Proceedings of the 1st International Conference on Multi-Area Simulation*. Angers (France): Frontiers.

Fauquet-Alekhine, Ph., Bouhours, G., Texier, J., Loret, A., Lahlou, S., & Granry, J. C. (2020). Training improvement through subjective work analysis: The example of radial puncture for arterial blood gas test. *Journal of Anesthesia* (accepted).

Fauquet-Alekhine, Ph, & Daviet, Fr. (2015). Detection and characterization of tacit occupational knowledge through speech and behavior analysis. *International Journal of Innovation, Management and Technology, 6*(1), 21–25.

Фоке-Алехин Ф., & Мартинес П [Fauquet-Alekhine, Ph, & Martinez, P.]. (2019, October 15–16). Повышение компетенций школьников на основе применения модели "воспринимаемый квадрат действия" [Improving the competencies of students through the use of the square of perceived action model]. конференции СОЦИАЛЬНАЯ ПСИХОЛОГИЯ И ОБЩ ЕСТВО: ИСТОРИЯ И СОВРЕМЕННОСТЬ, Москва [Conference *Social Psychology and Society: History and Modernity*, Moscow].

Fauquet-Alekhine, Ph., & Martinez, P. (2020). Cognitive task analysis to improve student competencies: A pilot study based on the use of the Square of PErceived ACtion model. *Teachers & Teaching* (submitted to).

Fauquet-Alekhine, Ph., & Lahlou, S. (2017). The Square of PErceived ACtion model (SPEAC model) applied in digital ethnography for work activity analysis: Performance and workers' perception. *Current Journal of Applied Science & Technology, 22*(3), 1–13. Article No. CJAST.34985.

Fauquet-Alekhine Ph., & Lahlou, S. (2020). Performance in collaborative activity: contribution of Intersubjectivity Theory. *Cognition, Work & Technology* (submitted to).

Fauquet-Alekhine, Ph., & Rouillac, L. (2016). The Square of PErceived ACtion model as a tool for identification, prevention and treatment of factors deteriorating mental health at work. *Journal of Mental Disorders and Treatment, 2*(3), 1–13. Paper #1000126.

Joensuu, M., Väänänen, A., Koskinen, A., Kivimäki, M., Virtanen, M., & Vahtera, J. (2010). Psychosocial work environment and hospital admissions due to mental disorders: A 15-year prospective study of industrial employees. *Journal of Affective Disorders, 124*(1), 118–125.

Judge, T. A., Bono, J. E., Erez, A., & Locke, E. A. (2005). Core self-evaluations and job and life satisfaction: The role of self-concordance and goal attainment. *Journal of Applied Psychology, 90*(2), 257.

Karasek, R. A., Jr. (1979). Job demands, job decision latitude, and mental strain: Implications for job redesign. *Administrative Science Quarterly, 24,* 285–308.

Le Bellu, S. (2016). Learning the secrets of the craft through the real-time experience of experts: Capturing and transferring experts' tacit knowledge to novices. *PISTES*, 18-1, http://pistes.revues.org/4685.

Mann, M. M., Hosman, C. M., Schaalma, H. P., & De Vries, N. K. (2004). Self-esteem in a broad-spectrum approach for mental health promotion. *Health Education Research, 19*(4), 357–372.

Mark, G. M., & Smith, A. P. (2008). Stress models: A review and suggested new direction. *Occupational Health Psychology, 3,* 111–144.

Nieuwenhuijsen, K., Bruinvels, D., & Frings-Dresen, M. (2010). Psychosocial work environment and stress-related disorders, a systematic review. *Occupational Medicine, 60*(4), 277–286.

Oomens, S., Geurts, S., & Scheepers, P. (2007). Combining work and family in the Netherlands: Blessing or burden for one's mental health? *International Journal of Law and Psychiatry, 30*(4), 369–384.

Ryan, R. M. (1995). Psychological needs and the facilitation of integrative processes. *Journal of Personality, 63,* 397–427.

Sheldon, K. M., & Elliot, A. J. (1999). Goal striving, need satisfaction, and longitudinal well-being: The self-concordance model. *Journal of Personality and Social Psychology, 76*(3), 482.

CHAPTER 6

Conclusions

Abstract This chapter briefly summarizes the contribution of the book in the paradigm of the Cognitive Task Analysis using the Subjective Evidence-Based Ethnography and its integration within the paradigm of Knowledge Management. It suggests the SEBE/SPEAC protocol as a prerequisite for occupational training as a relevant and efficient method to provide input data in the aim of defining the training and pedagogical objectives of training sessions by clearly identifying the needs.

Keywords Cognitive Task Analysis · Subjective Evidence-Based Ethnography · Knowledge Management · SEBE/SPEAC protocol

The SEBE/SPEAC protocol presented in this book originated from a general industrial problem related to the social phenomenon of "skills drain"[1] (retired workers leaving companies *en masse* sometimes even before the recruitment of newcomers). This phenomenon impeding mentoring, managers are seeking innovative solutions to train new employees and ensure a satisfactory level of competencies, especially in high-risk industries. From an industrial standpoint, in high-risk industries, the general question addressed what makes operational professionals competent in work activities.

[1] "Skills drain" not to be confused with "brain drain".

P. Fauquet-Alekhine, *Knowledge Management in High Risk Industries*, https://doi.org/10.1007/978-3-030-49213-7_6

In order to help newcomers elaborate competencies, the issue is thus to establish the following:

> What should be transferred from experienced workers to novices through training in the current social context of deteriorated mentoring within complex socio-technical systems? How to select what should be transferred? How to access experienced workers' competencies?

How does the SEBE/SPEAC protocol bring an innovative and efficient solution to this issue?

Firstly, the SEBE/SPEAC protocol is based on the relationship between knowledge, know-how, skills and competencies. Facing the absence of general consensus in the literature, we suggest a summary of this issue that does not claim to be the truth but to present appropriate considerations regarding the problems addressed: competencies are considered as an overall concept designating knowledge, know-how and skills where knowledge is a prerequisite to know-how and skills; skills develop from know-how in action with experience, where "experience" means being exposed to situations several times and at a certain frequency. We synthesized these inter-conceptual proposals through the Knowledge—Know-How—Skills model (KKHS model).

Secondly, the Square of PErceived ACtion model (SPEAC model) drawing competencies in action as a square made up of four poles—*Knowing to act, Wanting to act, Being able to act* and *Having to act*—was found to be the only way to describe competencies in action necessary to clearly identify what should be transferred from experienced workers to novices.

The SPEAC model structures a protocol to access competencies in action. Within the Cognitive Task Analysis paradigm, this is achieved by applying a Subjective Evidence-Based Ethnographic method (SEBE method). The SEBE/SPEAC protocol combines a first-person video recording of the activity followed by an in situ subjective interview (replay interview or RIW) questioning the four poles of the SPEAC model. The protocol was successfully tested and applied in individual and collaborative nuclear and medical activities as well as at school during a pilot study.

For each work activity analysed, the SEBE/SPEAC protocol showed significantly higher efficiency when compared with three other methods:

a better description of explicit knowledge and know-how was obtained, tacit knowledge and tacit know-how were identified while not detected with other methods and the cost of the analysis was reduced by 30%. The outcome of this method is to provide input data that can be used for training programmes when developing trainee competencies. This is concretized by the matrix of competencies.

Application of the matrices of competencies provided by the SEBE/SPEAC protocol used in the design of training programmes has been shown to contribute towards a significant improvement in results in terms of performance: a higher level of trainee satisfaction, greater improvement in activities in terms of performance, quality or safety indicators, as well as significant avoided costs. Applying the SEBE/SPEAC protocol provides benefits at two levels: (i) improvement in existing training sessions and (ii) renewal of the content of existing training sessions. "Renewal" is a key factor in successful training. Indeed, too often, training content and structure are unchanged for long periods of time while the needs may have changed due to work contexts changing; at the same time, refresher training often offers the same content as initial training. In fact, we suggest considering training like fashion: it must be seen as an "industry of change and renewal" as defined by Giorgio Armani (Baudo, 2015: 49); repeating training with the same content and structure can just bore trainees, reducing their level of interest (and thus their motivation) and their capacity to reactivate knowledge and know-how.

The matrices of competencies also demonstrated their usefulness in evaluation by associating one or more observables with identified knowledge and know-how.

In addition, the performance of the SEBE/SPEAC protocol was assessed by external experts during a two-week WANO[2] peer review at Chinon NPP: the process and organizational performances were assessed in depth. Experts identified the work done when applying the SEBE/SPEAC protocol on Reliability Practices in Operations teams as demonstrating "a new, higher level of excellence that would benefit other plants in the industry to emulate [...] [and] should be considered

[2]WANO is the World Association of Nuclear Operators. It gathers all industries worldwide providing electricity from nuclear energy. WANO undertakes periodically peerreviews in NPPs with the help of internationally renowned experts. WANO's assessment always makes reference.

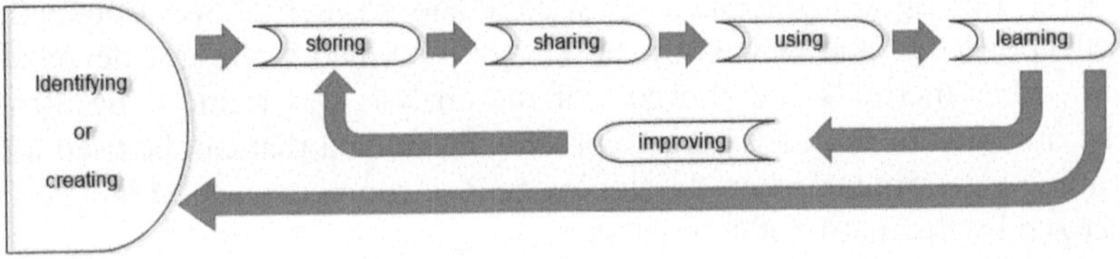

Fig. 6.1 Knowledge Management Cycle (KMC) model (Evans, Dalkir & Bidian, 2014)

as 'redefining' excellence" with a possibility of being "likely [to] drive change in the industry".

How does the SEBE/SPEAC protocol integrate Knowledge Management (KM)? Evans, Dalkir and Bidian's model of KM cycle helps to answer this question (Evans, Dalkir & Bidian, 2014). On the basis of the examination of several acknowledged KM models in more than one hundred KM contexts, the authors elaborated the Knowledge Management Cycle (KMC) model (Fig. 6.1): when a knowledge request is triggered in the organizational system, it is necessary to identify in which form it may already exist or whether it must be created; the results are stored within the organization in order to be redistributed when needed during a phase of sharing which may take a multiple of forms (e.g. formal or informal exchanges, collaborative activities, seminars, training) in the aim of being used in operational situations; during or just after the phase of use, the phase of learning is crucial as it is when the experience gained through the previous phases may be transformed into new knowledge that can foster the initial phase.

The SEBE/SPEAC protocol intervenes in the two first phases of the KMC model: identifying or creating is undertaken when analysing the activity and storing is materialized by the resulting matrix of competencies. The phase of sharing is illustrated in this book in Chapter 5 when using the matrices of competencies to design training sessions.

Furthermore, qualitative data and quantitative data were analysed to evaluate the level of acceptance of the SEBE/SPEAC protocol by workers. Conclusions were that workers did not perceive the protocol as constraining but found it innovative, efficient and interesting if applied to colleagues and other activities. The presence of the recording device that might stress the workers or change their behaviour is not seen as a problem: participants confessed that they were disturbed at the beginning of their activity but very soon forgot about the subcam when involved in the nitty-gritty of the activity.

We suggest that all companies concerned by the phenomenon of skills drain could benefit from the method presented here to improve their professional training. Three key points make the SEBE/SPEAC protocol of interest: its efficiency in detecting knowledge and know-how, its low cost and good worker acceptance. Moreover, we developed and tested a protocol for risk assessment when applying a SEBE method (including eye-tracking methods) with a hundred participants and seven different professions. The elaborated risk assessment protocol gave satisfactory results in terms of risk prevention and the time necessary for its application: no incident or accident occurred and the risk assessment took less than five minutes. The SEBE/SPEAC protocol may thus be applied safely in high-risk environments.

Finally, the SEBE/SPEAC protocol may be applied to the analyses of any activity or learning situation, including educational contexts. Beyond training, the SPEAC model has shown its ability to demonstrate the role of competencies in the analysis of deviations at work or in the analysis of psychosocial risks.

The potential of the recently developed SPEAC model has not yet been fully investigated. However, it is clear that the possibilities exceed the description presented in this book. For example, the exhaustiveness of matrices of competencies provided by the SEBE/SPEAC protocol can help to foster Artificial Intelligence algorithms whenever an activity is to be performed by robotic equipment. When taking an opposite perspective, it could allow the endangered craft trades to survive by compiling "jobtheques"; they would archive the subjective videos of realization of the activities for a subsequent or ulterior transmission of competencies.

References

Baudo, G. (2015). Giorgio Armani's staying power. *System Magazine, 5*.

Evans, M., Dalkir, K., & Bidian, C. (2014). A holistic view of the knowledge life cycle: The Knowledge Management Cycle (KMC) model. *The Electronic Journal of Knowledge Management, 12*(2), 85–97.

Appendix 1: Sample of Informed Consent

Reference study / Reference subject	.... / ....
Reference doc:	**ROS lign Cond informed consent (Eng) 01**

EDF

LSE Psychological and Behavioural Science

Activity Analysis «Operating Circuit Configuration» to Access Competencies of Performers

Informed Consent

A1 Purpose:
Access to what makes the performers' competencies when performing operating circuit configurations in order to improve the relevance of the specifications of the associated training.

A2 Participant profile:
Personnel involved in French nuclear power plants.

P. Fauquet-Alekhine, *Knowledge Management in High Risk Industries*, https://doi.org/10.1007/978-3-030-49213-7

A3 Procedure:

After carrying out specific risk analysis regarding the equipment used for the analysis of work activity, the worker in charge of the activity (e.g. field worker, operating pilot) is equipped with miniaturized video recording device. Sometimes, the work analyst may also be equipped with a miniature video recording device or may use a camcorder mounted on a tripod.

Work activity is recorded at the earliest.

What is recorded is then debriefed by the analyst only with participants during an interview in order to understand what was done and how. A possible additional information may be asked to colleagues who contributed to the activity.

An analysis follows the results which are submitted to participants for validation.

A4 Time commitment:

The total time required to complete the study should be the time of the activity.

A5 Recordings

Recordings are made by subcam (miniature camera mounted on glasses) or camcorder on tripod when performing the activity. The following debriefings are also recorded for later analysis for understanding and identifying what makes the competencies of the worker. These recordings and associated data are classified confidential by the analyst and are stored and used by him according to the code of ethics of his profession.

A6 Benefits/Risks to Participant:

The workers can identify areas for improvement in their professional practices and thus enhance their skills.

All participants contribute to the improvement of the training programme in general.

The only known risk for participants in this study is the misuse of data acquired. To reduce this risk, the recordings and associated data are classified confidential by the analyst and are stored and used by him according to the code of ethics of his profession.

The use of individual data is then integrated into an overall approach that does not identify the participants.

A7 Voluntary Nature of the Study/Confidentiality:
Participation in this study is entirely voluntary; participants may refuse to complete the study at any point during the experiment or refuse to answer any questions with which they are uncomfortable. They may also stop at any time and ask the researcher any questions they may have. Their name will never be connected to their results or to their responses on the questionnaires; instead, a number will be used for identification purposes. Information that would make it possible to identify participants will never be included in any sort of report.

A8 Cost, reimbursement and compensation:
Participation in this study is voluntary. There will be no supplementary income.

A9 Questions and contacts:
During the study and after, participants may ask any questions they may have about the study. If participants have questions later, they can contact:

Dr. Fauquet-Alekhine, Work Psychologist
Email: p.fauquet-alekhine@lse.ac.uk or philippe.fauquet-alekhine@edf.fr
Address: CNPE of Chinon-BP80-F37420 Avoine
Phone: +33247987804

A10 Declaration of consent:
The information above is read and approved.

Participant Name (*):	Name of analyst:
________________	________________
Date / Signature:	Date / Signature:

Thanks for participating

(*)Participants who wish to maintain some anonymity can use their initials (in agreement with the British Psychological Society Guidelines for Minimal Standards of Ethical Approval in Psychological Research).

Appendix 2: Set of Indirect Questions to Question the Speac Model and the Activity Goals

These statements may be used as indirect questions to question the four poles of the SPEAC model. During an interview, all questions must not be asked. It is suggested to tick a selection of questions per pole during the pre-analysis phase of the SEBE/SPEAC protocol. The selection is performed according to the analyst's assessment of their relevancy regarding the activity analysed. Ticking the questions during the pre-analysis phase allows the analyst to find quickly which questions must be asked during the replay interview.

Having to act

The tense to be used during the interview is present.

The direct positive question is: What do you have to do for such situation/activity/case?

The indirect questions may be:

- Which instructions are given, by who?
- Are you given particular instructions, by who?
- Which documents are given, by who?
- What are the written requirements/rules given?
- How would you define the activity you have to do?
- What are you expected to do, by who, by what?
- What a novice must do for such situation/activity/case?

P. Fauquet-Alekhine, *Knowledge Management in High Risk Industries*, https://doi.org/10.1007/978-3-030-49213-7

- What is the overall goal as defined by the order given for such situation/activity/case?
- What is the overall goal as defined by the organization for such situation/activity/case?
- What is the overall goal as defined by the prescription for such situation/activity/case?
- What is the overall goal as defined by yourself for such situation/activity/case?
- Do you establish for yourself particular rules to follow for such situation/activity/case?
- What is your own representation of what must be performed?

The direct negative question is: What don't you have to do for such situation/activity/case?

The indirect questions may be:

- What do others expect yourself not to do?
- What is expected to be avoided?
- What is forbidden?
- What were the rules missing?
- What do you forbid you to do?
- What a novice must not do for such situation/activity/case?
- Are you update of what some others do while must not be done?

Knowing to act

The tense to be used during the interview is present.

The direct positive question is: What do you know to do for such situation/activity/case?

The indirect questions may be:

- What are the prerequisites to know before performing such activity?
- What a novice must know for such situation/activity/case?
- If you were novice, what would you expect to be taught for such situation/activity/case?
- How do you know what is expected from you?

The direct negative question is: What don't you know to do for such situation/activity/case?

The indirect questions may be:

- According to the (sub)goals you defined earlier, what was the knowledge / know-how missing?

- What may be thought as a prerequisite in terms of knowledge or experience and be found useless afterwards?

Being able to act

The tense to be used during the interview is simple past.

The direct positive question is: What were you able to do for such situation/activity/case?

The indirect questions may be:

- Did you have all means at your disposal?
- What a novice must be able to do for such situation/activity/case?
- If you had been novice, what additional means would have been necessary?
- What kind of help could/should you expect from other professions?

The direct negative question is: What were not you able to do for such situation/activity/case?

The indirect questions may be:

- According to the (sub)goals you defined earlier, what were the means missing?
- What were the tools missing?
- What was the help missing?
- What was impossible to do?
- Which difficulties did you encounter?
- Are there things others did instead of you?

Wanting to act

The tense to be used during the interview is preterit.

The direct positive question is: What did you want to do for such situation/activity/case?

The indirect questions may be:

- Did you do all what you wished to do during this activity? What was it?
- What did you want to reach?
- What did you force yourself to do due to the fact that you were observed?

The direct negative question is: What didn't you want to do for such situation/activity/case?

The indirect questions may be:

- What did you want to avoid?
- What would you not have to do if you would be novice in the case?
- Do you feel you did anything you wanted to avoid?
- Are there things you did but think you should have let others do it?
- At this time of the video, is there anything you have done differently from what you planned to do?
- What did you avoid due to the fact that you were observed?

Goal-oriented questions during replay interview
The direct question may be: What is/was/are/were yours goal(s) for such situation/activity/case?

The indirect questions may be:

- For which reasons you do/did that?
- For which reasons you avoid that?
- What would you say here in this situation at this time to a novice colleague?
- Do you define (sub)goal(s) for the activity?
- What is your following objective at this time of the video?
- What are you about to do at this time of the video?

Appendix 3: Operational Communication at Work

Although psycholinguistic studies have been undertaken addressing speech and communication in the workplace (Cameron & Webster, 2005; Limaye, 1992; Roth 2004), or addressing style of communication (Chovanec, 2008; Dunkerley & Robinson, 2002), the literature is scarce regarding studies on communication between co-workers of a given work activity or about the study of its reliability. This type of communication is called "operational communication" in French nuclear power plants, but this expression can have other meanings depending on the field of activity considered. Organizational communication training websites suggest that operational communication is a form of internal communication in a company (ascending, descending or transverse) whose function is to organize and control the operation of the socio-technical system. Bojin and Dunan (2011) mention several aspects of operational communication: "to draw up the state of an issue, to defend an investment file, to present a strategy, to pose a problem to make proposals". Although these propositions seem to integrate the notion of "operational communication" as envisaged in French nuclear power plants, the scope of operational communication far exceeds them. In the military world, operational communication is "a command function applicable across the spectrum of military operations and at all operational levels" (Combelles-Siegel, 2002: 2 and 7). "Operational communication (COMOPS) is the collection of all activities carried out to communicate public information about a military operation or exercise" (DIA, 2007: 6).

P. Fauquet-Alekhine, *Knowledge Management in High Risk Industries*, https://doi.org/10.1007/978-3-030-49213-7

The same meaning is used for the management of health crisis by medical authorities (De Sa, Mounier-Jack, & Coker, 2009). In civil aviation, "Airline Operational Control/Communication (AOC) services involve data transfer between the aircraft and the Airline Operational Centre or operational staff at the airport associated with the safety and regularity of flights" (B VHF, 2005: 7). In the aerospace industry, operational communication is linked to hardware (satellites, radars, transmission systems) (Goodman, 2005) and rarely to verbal operational communication (Love & Reagan, 2013: 92).

In direct relation to work activities, the French scientific literature proposes the concept of "functional communication" [in French: *communication fonctionnelle*] introduced by Savoyant and Leplat (1983) and taken up by Falzon (1994). This concept concerns "communications directly looking at the content of the work done, excluding those that are primarily focused on human relations in the team, on the cohesion, on the influence processes, etc". Leplat (2001: 3) adds: "Communications can also be not directly functional. In this case, Grosjean and Lacoste (1999) speak of 'interstitial communications' aiming at 'maintaining or reinforcing the social link'". However, the name is confusing when it is translated literally into English. Indeed, the notion of "functional communication" concerns a completely different concept than that envisaged by Savoyant and Leplat. Larson (1978) states that "the term 'functional communication' refers to the skills and knowledge possessed by an individual, from which that individual's competence or effectiveness may be inferred". For Worrall et al. (2000), "functional communication is a concept that is embedded in the impairment realm, disability realm, or handicap realm" and the authors note that Hartley (1992: 265) defines it as "communication skills necessary for communicating adequately and appropriately within an individual's own environment, including independent living and consumer activities, interpersonal relationships, academics endeavours, and work-related activities".

The review of the Anglo-Saxon scientific literature leads to two proposals defining "operational communication": one appears in an industrial report published more than fifteen years ago (Rocky Flat Plant, 1995) suggesting that operational communications are "messages concerning the operation of the plant"; the other is more recent, in the Encyclopedia of Applied Linguistics (Johnson & Johnson, 2012) which defines "Operational communication" as "the combination of communication procedures, technologies, and language systems used for a range of operationally specifiable communicative purposes, working environments, or settings". On this basis, Garner and Watson (2007: 52) deal with operational communication in a medical environment and refer to operational communication research (see the book by Johnson & Garner, 2006) explaining that "This branch of applied linguistics aims to enhance the operational effectiveness of organizations such as the emergency services and transport authorities through developing and implementing efficient communication practices, specifically in relation to language use". In addition, they specify that "Its outcomes [of this research] are a series of recommendations for standardized language procedures relating to practices to be employed or avoided within the given context, which are enshrined in, for example, training programmes and communication manuals".

In spite of this, Dekay (2012) complained that "interpersonal communication in the workplace resembles a largely unexplored region". That is why it seems important to clarify the notion of communication in the context that interests us, the workplace. We must note that "to communicate" differs from "to inform" in that the former involves "reciprocity" (through dialogue) and "understanding of others" (by understanding the signifiers and also by understanding the other) (Zarifian, 2010). It is therefore a question of exchanging information and not of distributing it. We thus suggest the notion of "interpersonal operational communication" [in French: *communication opérationnelle interpersonnelle*], combining the definitions of the Anglo-Saxon literature for "operational communication" and the French literature for "*communication opérationnelle*" (communication within the company) and "functional communication" (communication in the work activity) when these definitions relate to the work activity:

> "Interpersonal operational communication" is the interpersonal communication between individuals in a field of work activities (ascending, descending or transverse communication) whose function is to organize and control the functioning of the socio-technical system, directly focused on the work activity which is being carried out or to be carried out, excluding forms of communication whose primary purpose is other than that of the work activity.

Another function of communication may be, for example, to maintain the link between interlocutors (Grice's cooperation principle [1975 and

1989] or Jacobson's phatic function [1960]). Thus, all cases of interpersonal communication at work are not necessarily operational communication even when they are technical: there may be informal exchanges between people at the coffee machine for example, far from the realization of the work activity, sometimes even not connected to any professional activity (talking about the holiday season or the weather for example).

The operational communication considered here is interpersonal because it concerns the exchange of information between individuals, either directly face-to-face, by telephone, SMS, email or Skype. The vectors of this type of communication cannot therefore be reports, notes or journals, for example, or minutes of meetings.

Therefore, interpersonal operational communication can take different forms including oral forms (e.g. telephone dialogue) or written forms (e.g. sms) and, for each, interpersonal operational communication may have different characteristics. For example, concerning the verbal form, if the action relating to the professional activity involves questions of safety, security or productivity in limited time, the operational communication can be shaped by a standard of secured communication (e.g. 3-way communication, see Fauquet-Alekhine, 2012a, 2012b, 2017a, 2017b). In this case, to be effective, interpersonal operational communication must be clear and precise, limited to operational issues at work and be as brief as possible. In practice, two workers repairing an engine in the field are involved in this form of operational communication, and the same workers, two days previously, while preparing the maintenance intervention, were also concerned with interpersonal operational communication.

References

Bojin, J., & Dunand, M. (2011). *Les outils de la communication écrite et visuelle.* Paris: Editions Eyrolles.

B-VHF. (2005). *Aeronautical communications—Functional principal and architecture.* UNISBG ref: D-06.

Cameron, A. F., & Webster, J. (2005). Unintended consequences of emerging communication technologies: Instant messaging in the workplace. *Computers in Human Behavior, 21,* 85–103.

Chovanec, J. (2008). Focus on form: Foregrounding devices in football reporting. *Discourse & Communication, 2,* 219–242.

Combelles-Siegel, P. (2002). *La communication opérationnelle et les opérations multinationales: comparaison des doctrines et pratiques américaines, britanniques et françaises.* Rapport de la Fondation pour la recherche stratégique.

De Sa, J., Mounier-Jack, S., & Coker, R. (2009). Risk communication and management in public health crises. *Public health, 123*(10), 643–644.

Dekay, S. (2012). Interpersonal communication in the workplace: A largely unexplored region. *Business Communication Quarterly, 75*(4), 449–452.

DIA-3.10.2 (Doctrine interarmées). (2007). *La Communication Opérationnelle.* Centre Interarmées de Concepts, de Doctrines, et d'Expérimentations. Ref: 297/DEF/CICDE/NP.

Dunkerley, K. J., & Robinson, W. P. (2002). Similarities and differences in perceptions and evaluations of the communication styles of American and British mangers. *Journal of Language and Social Psychology, 21*, 393–409.

Falzon, P. (1994). Dialogues fonctionnels et activités collectives. *Le Travail Humain, 57*(4), 299–312.

Fauquet-Alekhine, Ph. (2012a). Safety and reliability for nuclear production. *Socio-organizational Factors for Safe Nuclear Operation, 1*, 25–30. http://hayka-kultura.org/larsen.html.

Fauquet-Alekhine, Ph. (2012b). Use of simulator training for the study of operational communication—The case of pilots of French nuclear reactors: Reinforcement of reliability. *Socio-organizational Factors for Safe Nuclear Operation, 1*, 84–87. http://hayka-kultura.org/larsen.html.

Fauquet-Alekhine, Ph. (2017a). Psycholinguistic analysis of operational communication (Part I): The standard usage of communication in high risk industries. *Linguistics Journal, 12*(1), 86–109.

Fauquet-Alekhine, Ph. (2017b). Psycholinguistic analysis of operational communication (Part II): Prescribed communication for reliability in high risk industries. *European Journal of Language Studies, 4*(2), 27–40.

Garner, M., & Watson, M. C. (2007). Using linguistic analysis to explore medicine counter assistants' communication during consultations for nonprescription medicines. *Patient Education and Counseling, 65*(1), 51–57.

Goodman, J. M. (2005). Operational communication systems and relationships to the ionosphere and space weather. *Advances in Space Research, 36*(12), 2241–2252.

Grice, P. (1975). Logic and conversation. In P. Cole & J. Morgan (Ed.), *Syntax and semantics, 3: Speech acts.* New York: Academic Press.

Grice, P. (1989). Logic and conversation. In H. P. Grice (Ed.), *Studies in the way of words* (pp. 22–40). Cambridge, MA: Harvard University Press.

Grosjean, M., & Lacoste, M. (1999). *Communication et intelligence collective. Le travail à l'hôpital.* Paris: PUF.

Hartley, L. L. (1992). Assessment of functional communication. *Seminars in Speech and Language, 13*(4), 264–279.

Jacobson, R. (1960). Linguistics and poetics, In T. Sebeok (Ed.), *Style in language* (pp. 350–377). Cambridge: MIT Press.

Johnson, E., & Garner, M. (2006). *Operational communication: Theory and practice.* London: Palgrave Macmillan.

Johnson, E., & Johnson, E. (2012). Corpus analysis for operational communication. *The Encyclopedia of Applied Linguistics.*

Larson, C. (1978). *Assessing functional communication.* ERIC Clearinghouse on Reading and Communication Skills. Urbana, IL: Speech Communication.

Leplat, J. (2001). La gestion des communications par le contexte. *Pistes, 3*(1).

Limaye, M. (1992). Conceptual and methodological issues in organizational communication research: A comment on "categorizing professional discourse". *Journal of Business and Technical Communication, 6,* 488–490.

Love, S. G., & Reagan, M. L. (2013). Delayed voice communication. *Acta Astronautica, 91,* 89–95.

Rocky Flat Plant. (1995). *Conduct of operations—Manual Glossary.* Ref: PADC-95-02053. Rocky Flats Environmental Technology Site, http://www.lm.doe.gov/cercla/documents/rockyflats_docs/SW/SW-A-003002.pdf.

Roth, W. M. (2004). Perceptual gestalts in workplace communication. *Journal of Pragmatics, 36,* 1037–1069.

Savoyant, A., & Leplat, J. (1983). Statut et fonction des communications dans l'activité des équipes de travail. *Psychologie Française, 28*(3/4), 247–253.

Worrall, L. (2000). A conceptual framework for a functional approach to acquired neurogenic disorders of communication and swallowing. *Neurogenic communication disorders: A functional approach,* 3–18.

Zarifian, P. (2010). La communication dans le travail. *Communication et organisation, 38,* 135–146.

Index

P. Fauquet-Alekhine, *Knowledge Management in High Risk Industries*, https://doi.org/10.1007/978-3-030-49213-7

H

I

K

L

M

N

O

P

R

S

T

V

The manufacturer's authorised representative in the EU is Springer Nature Customer Service Centre GmbH, Europaplatz 3, 69115 Heidelberg, Germany. If you have any concerns regarding our products, please contact ProductSafety@springernature.com

Printed and bound by CPI Group (UK) Ltd, Croydon, CR0 4YY
05/10/2026
02228155-0002